PURE
HEARTED

MARK ONGLEY

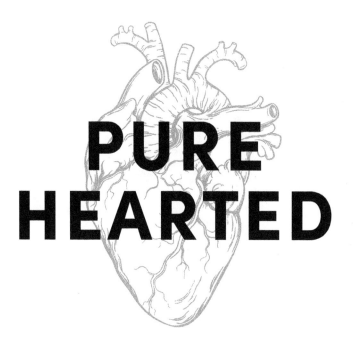

PURE HEARTED

BANDING TOGETHER
FOR SEXUAL WHOLENESS

Seedbed

Scripture quotations unless otherwise noted are from New Revised Standard Version Bible, copyright © 1989 National Council of the Churches of Christ in the United States of America. Used by permission. All rights reserved.

Scripture quotations marked ESV are from the ESV® Bible (The Holy Bible, English Standard Version®), copyright © 2001 by Crossway, a publishing ministry of Good News Publishers. Used by permission. All rights reserved.

Scripture quotations marked NIV are taken from the Holy Bible, New International Version®, NIV® Copyright © 1973, 1978, 1984, 2011 by Biblica, Inc.™ Used by permission of Zondervan. All rights reserved worldwide. www.zondervan.com The "NIV" and "New International Version" are trademarks registered in the United States Patent and Trademark Office by Biblica, Inc.™ All rights reserved worldwide.

Printed in the United States of America

Cover design by Nate Farro
Page design by PerfecType, Nashville, Tennessee

Ongley, Mark
   Pure hearted : banding together for sexual wholeness / Mark Ongley. – Franklin, Tennessee : Seedbed Publishing, ©2021.
      pages; cm.
      ISBN 9781628248333 (paperback)
      ISBN 9781628248340 (Mobi)
      ISBN 9781628248357 (ePub)
      ISBN 9781628248364 (uPDF)
      1. Pornography--Religious aspects--Christianity. 2. Sex addiction--Religious aspects--Christianity. 3. Sex--Biblical teaching.
      4. Sex--Religious aspects--Christianity. 5. Sexual ethics. I. Title.

BV4597.6 O54 2021   241/.667   2021931709

 Seedbed

SEEDBED PUBLISHING
Franklin, Tennessee
seedbed.com

Contents

Cycle Four: A Vision for the Church

Appendixes

Introduction

It was a warm summer night. I was a twelve-year-old, longing to step into manhood, and quite unable to sleep. Suddenly, light poured in through the window on the south wall. For some reason, the curtains had been left open, and I knew the light must be coming from our neighbor's house.

Our houses were just fifteen feet apart. Rising from bed, I peered through the window to see the open bedroom window of the neighbor girl—a blooming teen about to enter her senior year. Like mine, her window and curtains were open because of the warm summer air.

She walked past her window briefly. I could tell she was getting ready for bed. My heart raced. But because our windows were not directly across from each other, the angle of view limited what I could see. I waited for what seemed like forever, hoping for that forbidden glimpse. Eventually the light went out.

Greatly disappointed, I slipped back into bed. But my mind wandered to vague scenes of intimacy and pleasure. At that point in my life, I'd not seen explicit porn and knew very little of what to visualize, but I knew my heart was longing for something.

The next night I laid awake, hoping to see the familiar light streaming through my window. Dad and Mom finished in the bathroom, shut their door, and soon all was quiet. I waited. And then, at last, the light came on. I jumped up to the window. But again, only a few fleeting moments of her moving through her nightly routine. If I went to my sister's room, I reasoned, I could see straight into this girl's bedroom!

My sister had moved away, and her empty room was just a few creaky steps down the hall. Walking as softly as I could, I entered her room and gently pried an opening between two blades of the venetian blinds. But the girl was not there. The fear of being caught by my parents combined with my anticipation was exhilarating. But where was she? Spooked by a creak in the house, I quickly retreated to my room and gently latched the door. But again, I gazed through my window. Where was she? And why was I even waiting? Did I really expect her to walk naked in front of her window? She was probably changing in the bathroom.

Then it happened. I gasped as she walked by her window bare from the waist down. My only glimpse was her behind. *If only I was in the other room!*

As quickly as I dared, I slipped out of my room and into my sister's. But before I pried open the blinds, the neighbor's light went out. That was it! End of the show. But not the end of the story. My mind began to play it out over and over and over, adding a few details—at least the details that I, in my ignorance, could muster.

Kicking the Habit

That first glimpse of nakedness was mild compared to the eyeful most kids are receiving today. The Internet has opened a window to a world of pornography with a just few accidental clicks on a screen. Most studies reveal the average first exposure to be at the age of eleven. By age fourteen, 94 percent of teens will have had far more than just a glimpse.[1]

No doubt you, the reader, at this point in your life, have taken in far more forbidden views than you care to mention. For many people, childhood curiosity has grown into an obsession. Eventually, if left unchecked, it can become an addiction. Could this be true for you?

Whether your issues with lust are an occasional entanglement or a maddening bondage, this resource is designed to help you find freedom. In the past two decades, much has been written about the lure of porn and its addictive nature. A few defining principles have emerged that apply to all who struggle.

First, you cannot kick this on your own. For lasting freedom, you need some fellow travelers. And this is not news for sincere followers of Jesus Christ. Paul's letters are replete with admonitions to love, encourage, and serve one another. Basic Christian living was meant to be done arm in arm. This is especially true when seeking God's grace to get free of addictive behaviors.

---

1. See https://www.njherald.com/lifestyle/20180408/kids-are-seeing-porn -sooner-than-adults-think.

I have adapted some questions from a tried-and-true small-group resource of the distant past. In the 1700s, John Wesley formed groups of seven or fewer, and called them bands. As people banded together, they opened up the deepest secrets of their hearts and found God's grace flowing in from others. In this way, they found strength to live a pure life.

The band approach is making a comeback. Seedbed Publishing has their own adaptation of this model, scaling the numbers back to three to five folks, and using their Discipleship Bands app and the Daily Text as a hub for interaction. In fact, some of you may currently be in one of those bands.

The size of your group when using this material may be as few as two and as many as five. The key factor is confidentiality. Do you feel safe enough with the men or women in your group to open up fully about your sexual temptations and stumbles?

Another finding that is obvious from a believer's perspective is that *sexual obsession cannot be kicked without help from God.* In fact, Patrick Carnes, the leading psychologist on sexual issues, said, "healthy, successful sex and a well-developed spiritual life are inextricably linked."[2] This resource points you heavenward for God's touch of grace.

That heavenward gaze begins with seeking God daily through prayer and meditation. Don't underestimate this practice! One

---

2. Patrick Carnes, *Sexual Anorexia: Overcoming Sexual Self-Hatred* (Center City, MN: Hazelden Publishing, 1997), Location 376.

counselee told me that the most helpful practice in his recovery was using the divine office—an organized routine of morning and evening prayers, Scripture readings, and affirmations.

Yes, it may be out of your tradition to read written prayers and to recite creeds, but it is a useful tool for positioning people in God's transforming light and for correcting the worldly distortions they have regarding sex. The Scripture passages, both morning and evening, are chosen to correspond with each lesson's content. (See appendix C, "The Divine Office for Sexual Strugglers.")

Finally, as a counselor who has worked with sexual strugglers for more than fifteen years, I know the following to be true: *You cannot completely kick this without going deeper.* Root issues and past experiences need to be addressed. To that end, the practice of formational prayer has been absolutely transformational for many. Therefore, with each lesson, you will find instruction on how to lead each other through "prayer keys" in order to find greater freedom from your struggles.

Keep in mind that *kicking habits becomes easier once you reach ninety days clean.* Recent research is proving what alcoholics have known all along. Their mantra for newcomers has always been, "Get in 90 AA meetings in 90 days."

The Format

The design of this book is to facilitate an accountability band of three to five people of the same gender. If one member is attracted to the same sex, that should be fine. Temptation is temptation. In fact, the person with same-sex attraction might find it very healing to receive acceptance and love from hetero members of the band. But having more than one person of the same gender with such attractions will obviously complicate things.

Whether this is a new group or an already established discipleship band, once you begin this ninety-day journey, it should be a closed group. No newbies. And everyone should fully commit to the ninety days. This makes for a group where people feel safe enough to share from the heart.

This book contains thirteen lessons. If done weekly, of course, this will last a full ninety days. If you want to continue beyond that, the final lesson has suggestions for moving forward. It is likely someone will slip up along the way, so continuing the band will help everyone make it through the ninety-day window.

The Content

You may have noticed that the book is divided into four cycles, each one reflecting progress on your journey. Scattered throughout the cycles you will find general principles, theology, and specific sexual issues. These will be addressed in the sections titled "Windows of Grace and Truth." Here's the rationale.

First of all, let's be frank. The church in general has done a poor job of addressing sexual issues. In fact, our wranglings over homosexuality have pretty well landed us in a ditch, and the mud has spattered us all. The principles found in this text help to get us back on the path and moving in the right direction to overcome our addictive behaviors.

Principles to guide us, yes, but why theology? Because the cultural landscape has been shifting dramatically beneath our feet since 2015. That year began with the film adaptation of the runaway best seller *Fifty Shades of Grey*. Four months later, the Supreme Court legalized same-sex marriage. And that very same month, Olympian and reality TV star Bruce Jenner transitioned to Caitlyn. Since that pivotal year, chaos has ensued, and the distortions spilling out from this cultural shift feed sexual addiction. A clear and robust understanding of God's design for our sexuality is critical to finding freedom.

And you may find it odd that a resource geared toward addictive issues takes time to look at sexual abuse, adultery, and other matters. But the overlap on these issues is significant.

Much of the content in the "Windows of Grace and Truth" sections parallels my other book, *Into the Light: Healing Sexuality in Today's Church*. This text, however, stands on its own two feet. If you want to understand more fully the ground those feet are planted on, however, you can order the main text at www.seedbed.com.

Getting Started

So how does one get this rolling? First with prayer. Obsession with sex and pornography is entangled with darkness. There are forces that don't want you or anyone else to get clean. And so pray that God will bring together the right handful of members for this band. The ninety-day journey will be intense. It is not for the faint of heart.

Familiarize yourself with the content of the first meeting so that you can make clear to the others the level of commitment required. And once they have prayerfully committed to the process, order copies of this book, and schedule the first meeting. Prior to getting together, you all should have read this introduction and the section titled "Banding Together for Purity: The First Meeting."

Windows of Opportunity

One warm evening, King David was peering through a window of sorts. While walking on his rooftop, his eyes caught the form of a lady taking a bath. Soon she was taken to his bedroom. And after murdering her husband, she was taken as his wife.

Their son Solomon was heir to the throne, and he seemed to have also inherited Dad's proclivity to sexual sin. But as king of a growing empire, Solomon could marry any woman who caught his eye—and he did! Hundreds of them.

If the words of Proverbs 1–9 came from his pen, you can see evidence that he wrestled with his sexual obsessions. Not wanting to pass them on to his own sons, he repeatedly warned them about adultery. Chapter 7 describes his late-night musings as he peered out his own window. Hear the pleading of a father as you read these words to his sons:

> Say to wisdom, "You are my sister,"
>> and call insight your intimate friend,
> that they may keep you from the loose woman,
>> from the adulteress with her smooth words.
>
> For at the window of my house
>> I looked out through my lattice,
> and I saw among the simple ones,
>> I observed among the youths,
>> a young man without sense,
>
> passing along the street near her corner,
>> taking the road to her house
> in the twilight, in the evening,
>> at the time of night and darkness.
>
> Then a woman comes toward him,
>> decked out like a prostitute, wily of heart.
> She is loud and wayward;
>> her feet do not stay at home;
> now in the street, now in the squares,
>> and at every corner she lies in wait.

She seizes him and kisses him,
> and with impudent face she says to him:

"Come, let us take our fill of love until morning;
> let us delight ourselves with love.

For my husband is not at home;
> he has gone on a long journey.

He took a bag of money with him;
> he will not come home until full moon."

With much seductive speech she persuades him;
> with her smooth talk she compels him.

Right away he follows her,
> and goes like an ox to the slaughter,

or bounds like a stag toward the trap
> until an arrow pierces its entrails.

He is like a bird rushing into a snare,
> not knowing that it will cost him his life.
> (Prov. 7:4–13, 18–23)

Have you been that ox led to the slaughter? While sexual obsession has not cost you your life, it has likely damaged your marriage, contaminated your sexual intimacy, and plagued you with self-contempt. If it has become public knowledge, it has robbed you of respect from your children, friends, and peers.

Is your room darkened by despair? Is it cluttered with broken promises and unkept resolutions? Look carefully. Can you see light coming through your window? It could very well be the light of God, ready to liberate you from the prison cell of sexual obsession. Don't pass this vulnerability on to your kids and grandkids. Seize this opportunity, and band together with a few trusted friends.

PURE
HEARTED

Banding Together for Purity:
The First Meeting

inety days. That's the goal. For most of you, it is the goal for abstaining from pornography. Others of you may struggle with lust, sexual fantasies, or obsessive masturbation. For some, trips to clubs, bookstores, or hookups may be the thing. Regardless of the obsession, you are invited to take the journey.

Thirteen weeks. Can you hang on that long? Some of you have tried to stop before. Your secret or not-so-secret behaviors have been following you into your bedroom, hindering your ability to respond to your spouse, and leaving him or her feeling rejected.

Three months. It can seem like an eternity when you are in the fog of obsession. But it's really just a small slice of your lifespan to gain control over an obsession that could eventually rob you of reputation, honor, and true intimacy.

In fact, get this: If you can make it through the first ninety days, the rest of the journey just might get easier!

Recent neurological research reveals that significant rewiring of the brain takes place in the first ninety days of recovery. And many are finding that abstinence for ninety days not only lessens the pull of pornography, but restores one's ability to respond properly to one's spouse. Instead of needing edgier and kinkier visual extremes, they have been able to recalibrate, finding sufficient arousal from the one they love.

There are three elements which can enable you to power through these thirteen weeks:

- Connection with God
- Connection with Others
- Resolving Deeper Issues

Connection with God

Solar panels. Don't you love them? Maybe it's because I am always looking for ways to save a buck, but I think it's great to power my calculator and other small stuff from the God-given energy of the sun. No need for batteries or outlets. You simply have to aim the panel toward the light.

There is a God-given source of energy to help you power through these ninety days: his sustaining grace. God's Holy Spirit enters each one who has placed faith in Jesus Christ. But just like solar panels, we need to position ourselves before his healing light on a daily basis to receive his enabling. While there are many ways to turn our hearts heavenward, the tried and proven means have always been Scripture and prayer.

Yep, I can already hear sighs, groans, and moans. A few of you have been battling addiction for years and have been told to pray harder and read your Bible more. And you've found it a bit like a stationary exercise bike: furious pedaling and much fatigue, but the scenery stays the same. I get that.

But for these ninety days, I'd like you to make a subtle shift in how you view daily devotions. Simply think of it as putting out solar panels.

Some days the spiritual atmosphere around you and the clouds of your own emotions will make it seem as though you are gaining nothing. But grace is seeping through those clouds. Some days, however, the clouds part and the beams of his presence will noticeably fill your heart with hope and energy.

If you have a satisfying practice of daily devotions which readily connects you with God, great. If your intake of Scripture and prayer are providing conscious contact, simply try putting the panels out both morning and evening.

Note: Many are finding an ancient practice known as the divine office a tremendous means of looking Godward, and so I've included appendix C, "The Divine Office for Sexual Strugglers." This will probably be out of your tradition and comfort zone, but I encourage you to try it for at least two reasons. Let's start with the hardest to swallow:

Written Prayers: Yeah, not my tradition either. But these prayers are written in first-person plural: "we" and "our" instead of "I," "me," and "mine." This is healing tonic for the narcissistic, self-absorbed soul, and it unites us with the prayers of people around the world. This is subtle but liberating. And having a routine of the same prayers day by day provides a much-needed spiritual rhythm.

You are encouraged to pray them slowly and from the heart. Like a well-chosen greeting card which captures our sentiments for the one we love, these prayers capture our soul's deepest needs and faintest groanings.

The Psalms: The divine office keeps our nose in the Psalms throughout the month. These are sacred prayers that point our panels heavenward both morning and evening.

The Psalms have been the prayer book of God's people ever since the days of King David. Jesus quoted from them frequently. Even while languishing on the cross, he reached for Psalm 22:1 to put words to his anguish: "My God, my God, why have you forsaken me?"

The struggles of the psalmists will echo your own at times. In fact, the scriptures chosen parallel your journey through these ninety days. And as you read with an open heart, God's grace will seep through the clouds.[1]

---

1. Have a smart phone? Many discipleship bands are finding Seedbed's Daily Text a tremendous resource for daily interaction with Scripture that allows conversation among band members. See https://www.seedbed.com/daily-text-subscribe.

Connection with Others

We need each other. That's just the way it is. Yes, our culture exalts the hardened individuals who, through grit and determination, climb to the top of the heap. But the reality is that the greatest triumphs require a team.

Jesus had the Twelve, three of whom became especially close. Paul had Barnabas, and then others. Moses had Aaron. David had his thirty mighty men. And you, my friend, need a band of brothers (or sisters).

There is a healing and empowering dynamic that arises when two or three open their hearts to each other in the name of Jesus. First of all, Jesus promised to be right in the midst of such a meeting (see Matthew 18:20). And Christians have found much grace when two or three live life together with transparency.

Such groups were the initial building blocks of John Wesley's Methodist movement. These "bands," as Wesley called them, were three to seven people of the same gender who asked penetrating questions about their inner life. The following are an adaptation of his questions, shaped for our purposes as a band:

- What sexual sins have you committed since we last met?
- What temptations did you face successfully?
- How did you overcome those temptations?
- Did you do anything questionable that you are not sure was sinful?

Okay, I think I heard a collective gulp! Not so sure you want to pry open your secrets just yet?

While our weekly questions are based upon Wesley's model, it takes a little time to develop trust and to sense safety in a new group. This week, simply take note of these questions. Take the plunge only when you are ready. Perhaps in the next two weeks you will feel safe enough to entirely open the vault.

Yes, you can lie about your secrets. You've probably become quite good at lying, actually. But here's a simple question: *Do you want to get free?* If so, honesty with one or two others is a must. How can anyone help you if you continue to keep secrets?

This is the reason for closing the group to newcomers, limiting it to no more than five, and requiring take-it-to-the-grave confidentiality. Such an atmosphere provides the safety needed for full disclosure. And as you hear each other's secrets, there's a huge need to be compassionate and free of judgment.

In his excellent book *Surfing for God: Discovering the Divine Desire Beneath Sexual Struggle*, Michael John Cusick identifies three types of accountability. "Cop" accountability, as the name implies, is all about finding the facts and "arresting" behavior. This, of course, can lead to shame and discourage honesty.

"Coach" accountability is a bit better. In this approach, each one in the band helps the others by spotting weaknesses and sharing how they themselves have found improvement.

But what we are aiming for in these bands is "cardiologist" accountability—opening up from the heart. Not a cop standing over you, demanding you fall in line. Not simply a coach who can come off as a know-it-all. But fellow students of the heart, each seeking God's enabling.[2]

We know that as we confess our sins to God we find forgiveness. But James 5:16 urges us to confess our sins to one other "so that you may be healed." Healing that transforms—that's what we long for. View these questions as a time for confessing and finding healing, not for dumping and finding shame.

The part of the brain that is stimulated by sexual arousal is the very part that relates with people. This is a key reason for needing a band. Deep connection with others will help fill this aching void!

So for the first ninety days, *connect!* Every day! Whether it's a text, call, e-mail, or lunch meeting, find a way to connect daily with members of the band. In fact, search your app store for "discipleship bands" for helpful tools. And make sure initiating contact isn't falling on just one person.

Finally, if possible, meet in person weekly to go through the questions and prayer keys. If schedules or geography get in the way, meet via Skype or Zoom. Contrary to John Wayne, Frank

---

2. Michael John Cusick, *Surfing for God: Discovering the Divine Desire Beneath Sexual Struggle* (Nashville, TN: Thomas Nelson, 2012).

Sinatra, or other cultural icons, we cannot do this alone. We can't power our way through this. We need each other!

Resolving Deeper Issues

As a follower of Jesus Christ, you already know that the world has taken God's beautiful design for sexuality and turned it into a commodity. Distorted messages about sex permeate our culture.

What is not so obvious is how deeply this has contaminated our thinking as believers. It doesn't help that the church has been crippled by an awkward timidity on all subjects sexual. That is why these lessons include teaching on basic principles and theology to prompt us to discuss God's design for our sexuality.

In addition to equipping your minds, each chapter in this workbook will also equip you with prayer keys to help you begin to resolve past issues and connect you more deeply with God. Like a ring of keys to keep with you throughout the day, these prayers can be pulled out and used as each occasion requires.

Keep in mind that some of you may need to pursue counseling from someone trained in formational prayer. Others will find it helpful to locate a twelve-step fellowship to address their past. If difficulties continue, seek out a certified sex addiction therapist.

But the content found in these lessons and the use of prayer keys will be sufficient for many to make it through the ninety days and to continue on the path of freedom.

"No Man Left Behind"

If you've watched the movie *Black Hawk Down* or a similar military flick, you are familiar with this slogan. No one is to be left behind on the battlefield.

As a band of sisters or brothers, we are making a commitment to leave no one behind in their battles. And so this group may need to go more than three months in order for each one to reach his/her ninety days.

Are you ready?

Ninety days. Thirteen weeks. Three months.

It is a window of opportunity for significant rewiring which, by God's grace, will enable you to walk in greater victory over sexual temptations.

Band Discussion Questions

- What in this lesson stood out to you?
- Why does joining this band interest you at this time in your life?
- Have you been a part of similar groups in the past? How were they helpful? Or not helpful?
- What has been the most difficult challenge when it comes to putting out spiritual solar panels on a daily basis? What can be done differently so that you have more of God's grace to reach the goal of ninety days?

- What is the best way for us to connect with each other on a daily basis?

Prayer Key: Surrender of Sexuality

As this first meeting comes to an end, take a minute for everyone to silently read the following prayer. Then ask if everyone is ready to pray it out loud together.

And be sure to write down your starting date for your ninety days!

Lord Jesus Christ,

Thank you for the many times you have forgiven me for my sexual sins. Your grace and mercy are amazing. And yet I still struggle. I cannot seem to get free. I need your intervention!

Give me strength! Protect me from the evil one! Meet me day by day!

By your grace, I surrender to your purposes for my sexuality as defined in your Word. I renounce the world's message that sexual fulfillment is a right. I refuse to meet my emotional needs through ungodly relationships and sexual activities. I will look to you as the Source for the fulfillment of my desires and only to my spouse as the resource you have provided.

Enable me to reach ninety days free from viewing pornography, masturbating to fantasies, or meeting up with others for sexual encounters.

In the name of Jesus!

Amen!

Starting date of your 90 days: _____

Assignments

A key part of this thirteen weeks is gaining a grip on a sound theology of sexuality. It's a brainwashing of sorts. And our brains could certainly use a good scrubbing! So be sure to follow through with the reading assignment.

Read Lesson One: "God's Good Design."

Connect with your band of brothers (or sisters) daily. (Seedbed has an app that facilitates daily interaction around a daily scripture: see https://www.seedbed.com/daily-text-subscribe.)

Connect with God daily using appendix C, "The Divine Office for Sexual Strugglers."

CYCLE ONE

A Vision for Wholeness

Years ago, I had an aspiring writer proofread a booklet I had written about God's design for our sexuality. Having been raised in a strict Christian home and enrolled in a Christian high school, he had never heard a balanced and biblical explanation for God's good design for his sexuality. Upon returning the draft, he stated emphatically, "If I had read this chapter when I was in junior high, it would have saved me a *lot* of heartache."

This cycle lays out a vision for wholeness. It reshapes our vision according to God's design, helps us identify sinful patterns in our behavior, and shines light on the idolatrous mind games we play.

As you begin this journey as a band, keep in mind an important principle from author and teacher Terry Wardle: "I am responsible for me and accountable to you." Drill that into your thinking. You are *not* responsible for your band members' behavior. They are. And you are responsible for yours.

Day by day, encourage each other as you build relationships. Ask God to develop loving friendships with those in your band. And, like spectators at a sporting event, cheer one another onward toward the vision for wholeness. Then at your weekly meeting, ask the accountability questions with much grace, and answer them with gut-level honesty.

May God grant you much clarity as you gain a new vision for his wholeness!

God's Good Design

If you have made it through the last seven days without caving in to your sexual temptations, *hallelujah!* That's tremendous! Yes, I know, you have twelve more weeks to reach the ninety days, but the goal is attained one day at a time. You now have seven, so you are well on your way!

And if you stumbled, just get back up, dust yourself off, and keep moving forward. In fact, as you confess to your band, have them help with the dusting by looking you in the eyes and stating, "In the name of Jesus, you are forgiven!"

And don't view a stumble as starting from square one. You've made progress on the path. Learn a few lessons as you walk through the "Coaching One Another" questions and write down your new start date. Prayerfully move forward. Remember that you are part of a band of brothers (or sisters). We are in this together!

And what is the goal? Purity: consistent victory over sexual sin. Not freedom from all temptation, of course, but freedom from the behavioral ruts where we've been stuck.

So what does that look like? This brings up the subject of masturbation. What exactly is consistent victory, especially when the urge for release becomes so strong? Is it always wrong for a man or a woman to masturbate? Or are there other means for release? Many mature Christians have differing opinions on the matter.

If your convictions are firmly in place regarding this issue, great. Follow whatever guidelines you believe God has given you. But if you are still undecided, you can read my observations in appendix A. They may be helpful as you prayerfully hammer out your own convictions.

Windows of Grace and Truth

Down through the centuries, the church has pretty much been tight-lipped about sexual subjects. But this tendency is far from biblical.

From Genesis to Revelation, the Bible is clear and frank about God's wonderful gift of sexuality. Within its pages one finds observation, instruction, and inspiration, but never obsession with sexuality. And there's no cover-up when Judah, Samson, David, and others commit sexual sin. The consequences for their sexual lapses are clearly laid out—but so is God's amazing grace.

The very story of creation provides clues as to God's plan for our sexuality. In fact, one finds four purposes for God's design in those initial chapters of Scripture.

First of all, God created us as male and female to more fully reflect his image: "So God created humankind in his image, in the image of God he created them; male and female he created them" (Gen. 1:27). While each of us as individuals reflect the image of God, together as male and female the reflection is more complete.

The second purpose? Having kids. The very next verse contains a command: "Be fruitful and multiply, and fill the earth" (1:28). A command which, by the way, we have happily and amply obeyed!

The next two purposes for our sexuality arise out of a simple comment which God made: "It is not good that the man should be alone" (Gen. 2:18). And after creating a woman, the Scripture declares, "Therefore a man leaves his father and his mother and clings to his wife, and they become one flesh" (Gen. 2:24). And so, the third purpose for sexual union with another is simply to meet the deep longing for companionship.

Practically speaking, how does this one-flesh union meet this longing? Through a chemical called oxytocin. It's the glue that binds our hearts to another person. Even when you learn someone's name, shake their hand, and get acquainted, a little bit of oxytocin is produced and some bonding takes place.

When a mother gives birth or breastfeeds her infant, oxytocin is produced in large quantities, bonding the heart of mother and child. And when husband and wife come together in sexual union, there is a spike in the production of oxytocin, cementing together a bond of love.

This is why masturbation always falls short. So often the end feeling is loneliness as oxytocin is released in the brain, without a person there to connect with.

Finally, the fourth purpose also addresses this loneliness. The Hebrew word that is translated to mean sexual intercourse also translates as "to know." Genesis 4:1 says, "Now the man knew his wife Eve, and she conceived and bore Cain." The chief purpose of sexual union is to know and to be known by another human being. This again is a reason God designed us as sexual beings— to meet that deep loneliness which he described as "not good."

Hmm. Wait a minute. "Not good"? So the singleness of Jesus, Paul, and countless others who have remained unmarried either by choice or by circumstances is deemed "not good"? And yet, each single is given this sexuality like a loaded gun never to be fired, or a violin never to be played? What's with that?

In her wonderful book *Redeeming Sex*, pastor and author Debra Hirsch masterfully distinguishes between social sexuality and genital sexuality. There is an appropriate intimacy that our sexuality fosters which, if kept within proper boundaries, bonds us with others in ways that can be healthy and liberating. In this way, Hirsch asserts, Jesus was able to "create a space between himself and others where real love is able to flourish and where feeling passionate toward another doesn't have to lead to having sex."[1] Such bonding apart from genital expression is available to us, and can bring great blessing to all who are made in God's image.

God hardwired us for relationships, and our sexual design has deep significance. It sets us apart from all other creatures. In fact, scientists have noted that humans alone seek privacy when making love.[2] It is because our sexuality reflects the image of God, unites our hearts deeply with another, and opens us up to a mysterious knowledge of another human being. It is indeed deeply personal and altogether relational in nature.

Band Discussion Questions

- Can you name the four purposes for our sexuality? In what way does your sexual obsession run counter to God's intended purposes?
- Would you agree that the dominant feeling following masturbation is loneliness? What other feelings do you experience?
- Besides loneliness, what other unmet needs do you think people are trying to fill with sexual activity?

---

1. Debra Hirsch, *Redeeming Sex: Naked Conversations About Sexuality and Spirituality* (Downers Grove, IL: InterVarsity Press, 2015), 57.

2. William H. Masters, Virginia E. Johnson, and Robert C. Kolodny, *Human Sexuality*, 3rd edition (Glenview, IL: Scott, Foresman and Company, 1988), 651.

The Three Cs

Abstaining from pornography brings some degree of suffering. For some, the withdrawal symptoms are mild, but others actually endure symptoms similar to those coming off of drugs. The neurochemical changes can manifest with the following: "insomnia, anxiety, irritability, mood swings, headaches, restlessness, fatigue, poor concentration, depression, social paralysis and cravings."[3]

Withdrawal symptoms, however severe, do begin to fade day by day. And after ninety days, it will be much more manageable. Suffering prompts us to lean into Jesus. And as you lean into him, seek the support of the members of your band.

Accountability is drudgery unless we know someone has our best interests at heart. Perhaps today as you confess to each other, share if you are experiencing any of these withdrawal symptoms. Say heartfelt prayers for God's strength to endure.

- **C**onfessing to One Another

    — What sexual sins have you committed since we last met?
    — What temptations did you face successfully?
    — How did you overcome those temptations?
    — Did you do anything questionable that you are not sure was sinful?

---

3. Gary Wilson, *Your Brain on Porn: Internet Pornography and the Emerging Science of Addiction* (Kent, UK: Commonwealth Publishing, 2014), Loc. 1426.

Week by week you will also coach each other, learning from each other's victories and failures. So if someone in the band stumbles or even faces severe temptation during the week, these questions are valuable.

- **C**oaching One Another

   What made you vulnerable to temptation? Were you:

   Hungry?
   Angry?
   Lonely?
   Tired?
   Stressed?
   Bored?

   This forms the handy acronym HALTS-B.

- **C**leansing One Another

   Today you will learn the first prayer key. But as the weeks progress, you will have additional keys to choose from with which to cleanse one another.

Prayer Key: Renunciation

In my work with people battling sexual issues, I have found resistance from evil spirits. Now let's be clear. Evil spirits don't cause us to sin. They are not responsible for our problems. But they can certainly stir the pot, especially if they get a foothold.

In Ephesians 4:26–27, Paul warns us that harboring anger can "give the devil a foothold" (v. 27 NIV). In other words, certain persistent sinful behaviors can provide evil spirits a place to latch on to our souls, yielding them a bit of control so that they can jerk us around. The answer is not to cast out demons willy-nilly, but to first deal with the footholds.

So, in the example from Ephesians regarding anger, we remove the foothold by first repenting of the bitterness and forgiving those who have hurt us. Then we can brush off any remaining evil influence with a simple prayer of renunciation.

This prayer key can be used each time we resolve an issue or find some healing on the road to wholeness, even if we don't sense a demonic presence. For example, after asking God to forgive a sexual sin, you can simply pray, "And if any spirits gained a foothold in my life as a result of this sin, I command them to go in Jesus' name!"

In light of last week's prayer of surrender, take turns praying the following prayer:

Gracious God,

Thank you for forgiving my sexual sins. Thank you for the opportunity to surrender my sexuality last week, and for your grace to walk in victory. If any evil spirits had gained a foothold in my life through my sexual sins, I now command them to leave in Jesus' name!

Holy Spirit, please fill me. Take over this area of my life. In Jesus' name, amen!

Assignments

The next lesson includes insights into the dynamics of sexual addiction. Even if your issues don't seem to be an actual addiction, you may very well find yourself looking in the mirror. Are you a puppy dog? Or perhaps a predator? Be sure to follow through with these assignments.

Read Lesson Two: "Puppy Dogs and Predators."

Connect with your band of brothers (or sisters) daily.

Connect with God daily using "The Divine Office for Sexual Strugglers."

Puppy Dogs and Predators

Whew! This is taking a lot of your time! You have to read a chapter a week from this book. Then there's a weekly meeting where you have to open up your heart. Not to mention texting or calling someone every day! *Do you even have time for all of this?*

Press forward, my friend. No doubt you have spent far more time surfing the Internet or hooking up with partners at parks, beaches, and malls. And as the apostle Paul once wrote: "When you were slaves of sin, you were free in regard to righteousness. So what advantage did you then get from the things *of which you now are ashamed? The end of those things is death*" (Rom. 6:20–21, italics mine).

Simply remind yourself of how your cave-ins to temptation have heaped shame upon you and have brought death to your marriage, finances, career, and key relationships. They have even had an adverse effect on your brain! Pretty costly, really.

Windows of Grace and Truth

If you read the divine office last week, you noticed that the great beginning of creation came to a crashing halt. Adam and Eve listened to a crafty serpent, believing his lies and crossing the only line God had drawn in the garden sand.

In this act, they established a pattern of twofold disobedience, which even now we see played out in our sexual sin: *submitting* and *grasping*.

First, they looked to created things to fill their needs instead of relying on God. They took the advice of a serpent and believed that a piece of fruit would make them like their Creator. Actually, they had been given dominion over all created things, including serpents and fruit. But they submitted to those very things to try to meet their needs.

The second act of disobedience? Grasping. They reached out and took what was not theirs to take.

Pope John Paul II stated that if these newlyweds had simply waited, God would have eventually given them that very fruit. They could have received it from him in his timing.[1] But instead they grasped.

When it comes to sexual addiction, it seems we are either puppy dogs or predators. Puppies are playful and affectionate.

---

1. Christopher West, *Theology of the Body for Beginners: A Basic Introduction to Pope John Paul II's Sexual Revolution* (West Chester, PA: Ascension Press, 2009), 37.

They love to be petted and to have their bellies rubbed. So nice and cute—at least until they pee on your shoes. And yet some of us mimic that behavior in our obsession over sexual touch and stimulation. We lean into whoever or whatever will seemingly rub our bellies. This is not so nice. In fact, it is idolatry.

Viewing pornography is also submitting to and bowing down to a created thing to find our needs met. Instead of submitting to God and leaning into appropriate people in legitimate ways to fill our aching souls, we lean into the air-brushed images who will do and say whatever our pain-fueled fantasies cry for.

As for predators, they reach out and grasp what is not theirs to take from another. Or in the case of viewing pornography, the fantasy is one of dominating, inflicting, or taking advantage of another. Instead of receiving with an open hand what God has for them in God's timing, they exploit and cross boundaries. In some instances, we rightly call this abuse.

Certainly, there are times when these two forms of disobedience overlap. But, in general, they characterize our predominant ways of satisfying sexual desire. In a later lesson, we will see how Jesus Christ addresses this twofold disobedience on his journey toward Calvary. But, for now, consider the following questions.

Band Discussion Questions

- If you had to tag yourself as puppy dog or predator, which would it be?

- How does it feel at this moment as you peel and stick that label on your chest?
- What about that characterization mimics your first experience with sexuality? Were you drawn in as a puppy longing for affection? Or were you the one crossing lines and grasping?
- How does knowing that you fall into one category or the other help you understand yourself better? Does it give you a sense of direction for the road to healing?

The Three Cs

Shame keeps people in the closet. There are memories stuffed in the moldy corner of the closet that we hope no one *ever* finds. And yet, I'll bet there's a deeper hunger to bring them out into the light and find acceptance and grace.

As trust grows within your band, I hope you will find increasing freedom to allow others to peer into the dark corners of your closet. My bet is that they will lovingly call you forth, dust you off, and speak grace into your life. And the day will come when you will do the same for them. It's love, God's holy love, which bands us together.

Approach these questions with honesty and grace. Much grace.

- **C**onfessing to One Another

    — What sexual sins have you committed since we last met?
    — What temptations did you face successfully?

— How did you overcome those temptations?

— Did you do anything questionable that you are not sure was sinful?

• **C**oaching One Another

What made you vulnerable to temptation? Were you:

Hungry?
Angry?
Lonely?
Tired?
Stressed?
Bored?

• **C**leansing One Another

Before learning a new prayer key, have someone lead your band in prayer, thanking God for his forgiveness and praying for the healing work of the Holy Spirit to transform all puppy dog and predator inclinations.

Prayer Key: Unholy Images

When we consider God's purposes for our design as sexual beings, it makes the perversion of pornography and the message of the world that much more outrageous.

And yet those images . . . they've become imbedded in our minds. Whether from Internet binges, inappropriate movies, or past illicit rendezvous, those images are so very persistent! They pop up all the time! And they condition how we view women and men, don't they?

One young man agonized over his sex life. When intimate with his wife, he could not get aroused simply by being naked with her. To his disgust, only the images of pornography could get him excited. "If only I could get those pictures out of my head!"

His cry for help reminded me of a prayer I had learned years earlier from Leanne Payne, a pioneer in ministry to the sexually broken. And so I prayed with this young friend, and we were both astounded at what God did! The effect of that prayer was powerful.

This prayer is so very simple and yet profound. In fact, you may want to do this each time someone in your band slips up. Two people are needed: one to lead and the other to receive. Begin with both of you praying quietly, presenting yourselves before the Lord, praising God, and silencing the enemy:

Gracious God, we thank you for the forgiveness that comes through the cross of Christ. Your mercy is never ending. You are such a loving Father. Thank you also for the authority that is ours over the enemy. And so in the powerful name of Jesus, we command any evil spirits that might be present to be silent. We bind you in Jesus' name. You cannot interfere with the work of the Holy Spirit as we seek God's grace.

The recipient is then instructed to visualize a cross. It can be a cross he or she has seen before, or it may simply be an image that comes to mind. Sometimes holding a small cross in their hands can assist with the visualization.

When they see a cross, instruct him or her that they don't need to do anything except keep their eyes upon the cross. The leader then uses the following commands to remove the images:

In the name of Jesus, I command all unholy images to come up and out and to go into the cross of Christ. You cannot resist! You must come up and out and go into the cross. The Lord Jesus is cleansing this person's temple. Therefore, come up and out and into the cross of Christ!

Repeat this command again and again, checking in occasionally with the recipient to see if something is happening. If not, ask permission to lay a hand on their head or shoulder, and continue with the commands.

When they think the work is complete, have the recipient repeat after you the following prayer:

Gracious God, thank you for removing those images! And if any evil spirits had a foothold in my life as a result of those images, I now command them to go in Jesus' name! Holy Spirit, fill me. In Jesus' name, amen.

Finish praying by anointing the person with oil, and praying for God to seal the work.

Then debrief a bit. Ask what they saw. Over time, you will be amazed with the similarities in the pictures people see.

Assignments

Read Lesson 3: "Fantasy and Imagination."

Connect with your band of brothers (or sisters) daily.

Connect with God daily using "The Divine Office for Sexual Strugglers."

Fantasy and Imagination

One of the most challenging and exciting opportunities I have is speaking to youth groups about God's design for our sexuality. Challenging, because they have been inundated with the world's message about sex being the center of the universe. Exciting, because I love seeing the lights go on in their eyes when they discover God's true purpose for his design.

I summarize that purpose with one word: *connection.* I repeat it over and over. We are relational beings, and God has given us the gift of sexuality so that we might more deeply connect with one other person. That's it.

The world so clearly has twisted this message, stating that we are sexual beings with a *right* to sexual fulfillment. And if a spouse is lacking, then love the one you're with.

Remember that sexuality is a created thing. It lasts only as long as we are walking this earth. And its purpose is deep bonding, connection, and relational fulfillment. In heaven our oneness with God and others will render sexual encounters as a dim memory.

Windows of Grace and Truth

Becoming one flesh, uniting soul with soul, is one of God's purposes for his design of sexuality. Bonding as one flesh is a process that starts when someone catches our eye and captures our heart. We call it "falling in love."

It's the greatest feeling in the world, isn't it? A cocktail of chemicals is splashing upon our brains as we enter this sublime obsession. All we can think about is that face, smile, voice, body shape . . . If ever love is blind, it is when we are falling in love. And God chuckles.

During this season of blindness, it is God's plan that we join with this amazing person in a covenant, and then have our first sexual experience while we are gaga for each other. And so our first experience should be one where we are going out of our way to please, affirm, and serve one another within the security of a sealed commitment. That was the plan, anyway.

By following God's design, that first experience should have been absolute ecstasy. It should have been about us freely receiving tender, exciting, extravagant stimulation, and climax— and willingly giving the same to the one we are crazy about. That's what *should have been.*

Those who study the science behind those ooey-gooey feelings make it clear—they last only two years. Then we return to our right minds. Then it is that we begin to wonder, *Hey, what happened to the magic? Doesn't this person love me anymore?* Physical touch becomes less frequent and has fewer fireworks. We feel less like God's gift to the opposite sex. So is something missing? What's going on?

Infatuation has given way to true love. Obsession has become for better or for worse. And God smiles.

The wowie-zowie stage was wonderful. It was a chemically induced phase of giving and receiving extravagant love. But as exciting as infatuation is, there's a deeper longing, isn't there? We all want to be loved and accepted unconditionally till death us do part.

Falling in love creates wonderful memories we can savor the rest of our lives. That's God design.

But there is still a part of us that hungers for that blindness, where someone looks at us as though we are the best thing walking on two legs. A hunger remains for sex with a perfect ten that is passionate. Someone who willingly lavishes sex that communicates we are all that and *more*.

If we have any bent toward addiction, this is when we can begin to stroll down that destructive path of sexual fantasy. Instead of savoring what we once had with our spouse and the contentment of our present bond, our minds wander elsewhere.

Isn't that the appeal of pornography and one-night stands? Isn't it that longing for blindness, when the one we are with looks like a swimsuit model and they look at us the same way? Where anything we desire for sexual delight is granted with a smile? It's visual cotton candy that delights our taste buds, but leaves us empty and sick to the stomach.

God's design for sexuality was not for endless orgasm and constant stroking of our ego. It was meant for connection and an expression of true love. *True love.*

Yep, God is chuckling when the two years of blissful blindness fade. We wake up from the dream world and wonder, *What happened? This person's not a swimsuit model after all!*

Like a drug addict trying out crack, could it be you are searching for that first high? As you surf the net, looking for eye candy, are you trying to recreate a moment when someone was gaga for you and willing to say and do whatever rang your bell? It's a chasing after phantoms, really.

What we truly long for, however, is a loving touch from another who is committed to us no matter the wrinkles, sags, thinning hair, or failing performance. For better or for worse . . . and that's when God beams with pleasure.

Band Discussion Questions

- What do you remember about your own season of falling in love? How blind were you?
- Do you have a memory of an early sexual experience with your spouse that seemed deeply fulfilling? Without sharing

the details of that experience, does it seem that it could be a memory to savor, replacing the online fantasies?

- Is it possible, or even practical, to savor the memory of that early sexual experience instead of grasping for fantasy? Discuss how this might play out.

- And if you are single, share what frustrates you about this lesson. The content describes God's ideal. Does it add any insight to help you in your struggles?

The Three Cs

In some traditions, confessing sins to another is considered a sacrament. In other words, they see it as a *means of grace*, or a way of receiving God' strength or healing. Let that be your anticipation as you step into these questions.

- **C**onfessing to One Another
    — What sexual sins have you committed since we last met?
    — What temptations did you face successfully?
    — How did you overcome those temptations?
    — Did you do anything questionable that you are not sure was sinful?

- **C**oaching One Another

    What made you vulnerable to temptation? Were you:

Hungry?

Angry?

Lonely?

Tired?

Stressed?

Bored?

• **C**leansing One Another

What prayer keys would be helpful for you today? Surrender of your sexuality? Removal of unholy images? Renunciation of spirits? Take time to pray with each other.

Prayer Key: Renouncing Objectification

Likely you are well familiar with how pornography affects our view of the opposite sex. "Objectification" is the official term, and the effects are multiplied many times over. It dehumanizes, making people simply an object to be used. Devaluing is another result, causing us to view others as subservient to our needs, desires, and fantasies. For men, it can foster misogyny, the hatred of women, leading to many unconscious forms of demeaning others.

Of course, like many distortions, it is easier to spot this speck in others' eyes and not see the plank in our own. And some don't recognize this distorted view until it finally begins to lift, as in, "Hey, I'm not picturing women with their clothes off anymore!"

Mainstream media certainly adds to this distortion with how women and men are depicted in ads, movies, etc. But for pornography users, objectification is mainly the result of repeated exposure to photoshopped bodies and whacked-out videos portraying people as objects for our orgasm.

Have you noticed how objectification has wounded others? For decades women have scorned themselves for the slightest wrinkles, the faintest sagging, and the remnants of post-pregnancy belly fat and stretch marks. Increasingly, it seems, young men are becoming obsessed over less-than-chiseled abs and unwanted body hair.

The brunt of these body blows hit our spouses. While they may be blind to this objectification in the early years, they eventually notice when we no longer watch them undress. It eventually dawns on them that sex has become more about climax than connection.

This ninety-day journey has included prayers for the surrender of our sexuality and the renouncing of demonic influence. Join together as a band to renounce idolatrous objectification of people as your means of finding sexual pleasure. The following prayer will open your souls to the sanctifying work of the Holy Spirit and the renewal of your minds.

Glorious God, maker of all that is good, forgive me for idolizing bodies and body parts, using them for my fantasies and selfish stimulation. I renounce objectification in Jesus' name. Dust me off from

> *those spirits which prompt this activity. And renew my mind by the sanctifying work of the Holy Spirit. In Jesus' name, amen!*

And in the future, each time you are tempted to undress someone with your imagination, simply cry out to God, "I renounce objectification in Jesus' name!" And then, if married, thank God for your spouse.

Assignments

Read Lesson 4: "The Box, the Path, and the Circus."

Connect with your band of brothers (or sisters) daily.

Connect with God daily using "The Divine Office for Sexual Strugglers" as usual.

A Perspective on Slipups

Years ago I heard about an unusual experiment. A muskellunge, an aggressive freshwater fish, was placed in a tank with some of his favorite edibles. Scientists (or, perhaps, federally funded folks who like to torment fish) placed a glass wall in the middle of the tank, separating the hungry "muskie" from its delectable delights.

Repeatedly, the large fish swam furiously toward the small school, only to slam his jaws into the invisible barrier. Eventually he gave up and became motionless.

At this point the federally funded fish taunters removed the glass wall. The smaller fish could swim within inches of the muskie, while he remained still, starving to death.

You may have all the sympathy in the world for that big fish. You have swum with newfound zeal toward the goal of sexual purity, only to hit that wall *again*. It becomes a matter of embarrassment week by week as you meet with your band.

Don't give up! Take note of any progress you've made. Have you put together a string of clean days longer than any time in the past? Praise God! Aim for more! Continue to press forward toward the ninety-day goal, seeking God's strength and healing. And hang in there until everyone in the band hits day ninety.

Slipups do not disqualify us. As you switch to the next cycle of divine office readings, you will note Moses' murder, Samson's chaos, and David's colossal collapse. And yet God used them in spite of their mess-ups to prepare the way for the Messiah.

Continually seek the filling of the Holy Spirit to be empowered by his holy love. Confess readily your faults and failures. And may God use the encouragement of your band to bolster your resolve.

The Box, the Path, and the Circus

Has anyone in your band had a slipup? It wouldn't surprise me. Overcoming this obsession can be like mud wrestling with a pig. Once you think you have a firm grip, you can lose your footing and slide back into the ooze. But stay in the fight!

Your band meeting should be a shame-free zone. At its roots, shame is about identity. It says, "What kind of sick person keeps going back to this mud hole?" And yet, that very same sense of shame can also feed one's obsession and foster hiding. So using shame as an accountability stick to keep each other in line is counterproductive.

Looking at someone with compassion can be a healing moment if done with love. If someone has slipped back into the muck, look them directly in the eyes and say, "Hey, we're with you! We are all going to reach the ninety-day goal! God forgives! We will keep praying! Press on!"

Windows of Grace and Truth

Did you read about Simon the Pharisee in this week's divine office readings? In this story is a principle which is absolutely liberating—the box, the path, and the circus.

The Pharisees were the religious police of the day. They were Johnny-on-the-spot whenever someone failed to follow the Jewish laws and traditions. They drew the lines carefully and clearly, making sure everyone stayed within their box. And if someone crossed the lines? You can easily imagine the judgmental stares.

This police duty included evaluating new teachers. So, when Simon invites Jesus and his disciples for a meal, his aim is not to be hospitable and caring. Nope. He wanted to see whether or not Jesus fit into the box.

Then the unexpected happened. A woman who was a "sinner" walked into the dining room, knelt at Jesus' feet, and began weeping. Her sin? Uh, everyone assumes it was of the sexual variety. Instead of fitting in the box, this girl's been living at the circus, and everyone knows it.

And what a mess she makes! Jesus' dusty, dirty feet are now being doused with enough tears to actually wash them. Add to this the stringy stuff that comes out of the nose when one weeps this much, and you have a slimy, muddy mess. And so she begins to wipe his feet, not with a towel, *but with her hair!* On top of that—literally—she kisses his feet. The final touch? Anointing his feet with a costly, scented ointment.

Simon quickly connects the dots. Jesus cannot be in the box. No prophet of God would allow a woman like *this* to make such a scene. The tears, slime, muck, grimy hair, and crazy kissing from a circus freak confirm it.

And yet here comes the precious and liberating word of the path.

Jesus reads Simon's mind and asks a few questions, all of which related to the customs of welcoming guests. Did Simon have someone wash Jesus' feet? No, but she washed them. Did Simon greet him with a kiss on the cheek? No, but she lavished her kisses on dirty feet. Did Simon anoint his head with oil? No, but she anointed his feet with costly ointment. And what was the point of these questions? She was forgiven much and so she loved Jesus much.

Boom! This hospitality quiz and its conclusion blow Simon's box apart. This young prophet is telling him that the out-of-the-box woman is closer to the kingdom than Simon himself!

Our life with God is not about a box. It is not about behavior containment. Not at all. It is about a path. A journey with one we are learning to love more and more. And the further down the path we travel, the more our hearts are transformed. The more we want to live holy lives that please our Savior.

Keep this firmly in mind: the repentant addict is closer to God than any rule-keeper glaring at you from the box.

If you slip up, it doesn't mean you've gone to the circus. You have simply stumbled upon the path. You've gotten a bit soiled, of course, but let your band of sisters (or brothers) wash off the dust with confession and prayer. Link arms with Jesus and take another step down the transforming path.

Band Discussion Questions

- Can you give examples of when your sexual failures have banged into the walls of a box-type of ministry?
- What would you say is the difference between using shame to keep people in line and the role of biblical rebuke? See if Galatians 6:1–5 is helpful.
- When it comes to sexual temptation, what would be the difference between a slipup and a trip to the circus?

The Three Cs

In a previous week, I referred to an addict's propensity to lie. The judgmentalism found in the box only adds to that tendency. Be mindful that we are people of the path as you again answer the following questions. A slipup is not the same as a trip to the circus.

- Confessing to One Another

    — What sexual sins have you committed since we last met?
    — What temptations did you face successfully?
    — How did you overcome those temptations?

— Did you do anything questionable that you are not sure was sinful?

• **C**oaching One Another

What made you vulnerable to temptation? Were you:

Hungry?
Angry?
Lonely?
Tired?
Stressed?
Bored?

• **C**leansing One Another

What prayer keys would be helpful for you today?

Prayer Key: Centering Prayer

A fantastic book on pornography addiction is Michael John Cusick's *Surfing for God: Discovering the Divine Desire Beneath Sexual Struggle.* For Cusick, the absolute number one, most helpful practice in his recovery has been centering prayer.

As North Americans, we are all about fixing and doing. With sexual slipups, the first question is often, "What do I have to *do* to get free from this obsession?" But centering prayer is about *being*, not doing. It is built around Psalm 46:10: "Be still, and know that I am God!" That's it. Period!

It is simply sitting in a balanced and comfortable position, closing your eyes, and meditating upon the fact that you are in Christ, and he is in you. He is right in front of you; as close as your very breath.

Yes, that can seem maddening. Thoughts will flow in and out of your mind repeatedly. But when they do, simply speak a phrase that recenters you, such as:

- *Jesus!*
- *Be still!*
- *I am his!*
- *He is here!*

This is the epitome of the phrase, "Less is more." We want to achieve our freedom by rigorous effort and well-worded prayers. But quieting ourselves in the presence of God transforms us. It absolutely changes us bit by bit by bit.

Most recommend twenty minutes each day. That, however, can be an intimidating commitment for most. Start small and add minutes as you go along. Set an alarm so that you don't have to keep looking at the clock.

Perhaps the following assignment is a good starting point for you.

Assignments

Read Lesson 5: "The Dynamics of Adultery."

Connect with your band of brothers (or sisters) daily.

Connect with God daily using "The Divine Office for Sexual Strugglers" as usual.

Practice five minutes of centering prayer for five days.

The Dynamics of Adultery

I've got one word for you, Mark: Run!" It was the best advice I could have received.

The previous evening, I was approached by someone. She had been flirting and winking for months, but that night she had finally declared her intentions. "I've had affairs before. No one has ever found out. And right now all I can think about is being in your arms!"

I couldn't have been more vulnerable. Week by week you ask each other the HALTS-B questions. I wasn't hungry or bored, but the A-L-T-Ss were through the roof! Severely tempted and scared out of my skin, I had skipped my office hours and had gone for a bike ride on a wooded trail. There it was that I called one of my dearest friends and heard his warning: "Run!"

And so I ran. My next call was to this lady, telling her in no uncertain terms that we were never going down this adulterous path. Later that day, I reached out to friends and colleagues, asking for their prayers and accountability.

Thank God for that one word: "Run!"

Windows of Grace and Truth

Last week we learned a key principle: the box, the path, and the circus. My guess is that most of you grew up with a boxed mentality. Usually we call it "legalism." It is distorted thinking that clouds our judgment. Like carbon monoxide, it can have a deadly effect without even being detected.

Take the matter of adultery. Where is the line that one crosses to commit adultery? Does connecting with an old flame via Facebook qualify? Are sexting or sending naked selfies really a violation of the seventh commandment? The box maintains, however, that if you didn't climb in bed, no harm, no foul.

Imagine that you are drinking a glass of tap water, and suddenly someone shouts, "Hey, careful! That water's *adulterated!*" After spitting it out, you'd ask for the details. Did arsenic or some other poison pollute the water?

And so it is with adultery. It is not a line that is crossed, but a matter of pollution.

Remember the four purposes for our design as sexual beings? One of them was about bonding, or becoming "one flesh" with our spouse. Adultery happens when our bond with our spouse begins to be polluted by bonding with another.

While bonding culminates in sexual climax, the process of bonding begins long before that. Bonding actually begins when your eyes fasten upon the body of another, and your mind begins to wander.

And this falls right in line with how Jesus addressed the seventh commandment: "You have heard that it was said, 'You shall not commit adultery.' But I say to you that everyone who looks at a woman with lust has already committed adultery with her in his heart" (Matt. 5:27–28).

In saying this, Jesus was not drawing a new line for the box, but rather telling the crowd that it's not about the box at all. It's not a matter of following laws, but following *him* along the path. Far from conformity to a list of rules, it is about transformation of the heart.

The pull of emotional adultery is so very strong. The many unmet needs of your past and present have created a thirst. But like sips from a polluted well, this drink will cause you to soon become deluded and irrational. You start consuming it, but eventually it consumes you, leading to ruin. Note the warning from Proverbs 5:

Drink water from your own cistern,
    flowing water from your own well.
Should your springs be scattered abroad,
    streams of water in the streets?
Let them be for yourself alone,
    and not for sharing with strangers.
Let your fountain be blessed,

and rejoice in the wife of your youth,

a lovely deer, a graceful doe.

May her breasts satisfy you at all times;

may you be intoxicated always by her love.

Why should you be intoxicated, my son, by another
woman

and embrace the bosom of an adulteress? (vv. 15–20)

Notice the shift from water to wine in verses 19 and 20? Falling in love is not only refreshing, but intoxicating. It quenches a thirst, but can also blur judgment.

A few of you in the band, no doubt, have been sipping from the wrong well. Maybe it has been reconnecting with an old flame on Facebook or hooking up with a dating site fling. The first few sips have felt good going down.

But the water is polluted. It will lead to ruin. Look to God for deliverance, and take my friend's advice: *"Run!"*

Band Discussion Questions

- What stood out to you from this lesson?
- To what degree do you think your view of adultery was influenced by the box?
- Are you currently involved in an inappropriate relationship with someone?
- How can we help you to make an exit out of this relationship?

The Three Cs

Just a reminder about confidentiality. If someone is willing to open up their heart and confess to emotional adultery, you can cause a world of hurt if you blow the whistle. In fact, it may well bring your band to an end.

- **C**onfessing to One Another

  — What sexual sins have you committed since we last met?

  — What temptations did you face successfully?

  — How did you overcome those temptations?

  — Did you do anything questionable that you are not sure was sinful?

- **C**oaching One Another

  What made you vulnerable to temptation? Were you:

  Hungry?
  Angry?
  Lonely?
  Tired?
  Stressed?
  Bored?

- **C**leansing One Another

  What prayer keys would be helpful for you today?

Prayer Key: Breaking One-Flesh Bonds

In Lesson 1, we read about the four purposes of God's design for our relationships. One way in which God addressed Adam's loneliness was through a one-flesh bond with a partner.

Bonds are formed with people all of the time. Most of them are appropriate. Some . . . *not so much!*

In my book *Into the Light*, I provide a description of the twelve steps of bonding. Beginning with eye to body, as described in today's lesson, it ends with the final step of genital to genital. Regardless of how many steps you have taken with a person, those bonds endure and have an effect. Our hearts are warm toward that person. Hence it takes little effort to reconnect with those feelings. For example, have you ever noticed the feelings that awaken when you see that old high school sweetheart?

But if you are willing, those bonds can be broken. You have authority in the name of Jesus to sever those bonds with a command. The following prayer has proven effective for many:

Lord Jesus Christ, forgive me for cherishing unhealthy emotional bonds with others. I am willing to break those bonds. Please reveal to me the names and faces of all those with whom I need to break bonds.

At this point, simply listen to see what names and faces come to mind. Take as long as you need. But as each name or face appears, simply state the following:

In the name of Jesus, I break the bond formed with that person!

Once the process seems complete, pray a prayer of renunciation, such as:

Thank you, Jesus, for your forgiveness for cherishing unhealthy bonds. And if any evil spirits had footholds in my life as a result of those bonds, I command those spirits to go in Jesus' name! Amen!

Assignments

Read Lesson 6: "Feeding Circus Monkeys."

Connect with your band of brothers (or sisters) daily.

Connect with God daily using "The Divine Office for Sexual Strugglers" as usual.

Practice ten minutes of centering prayer for five days.

Feeding Circus Monkeys

Back in the 1960s, my protective parents monitored my TV watching fairly closely. The only nightmare-producing scenes I viewed were of the flying monkeys on *The Wizard of Oz.* Both fascinating and frightening, I can still see those blue-faced minions landing in the forest, capturing Dorothy, scooping up Toto, and knocking the stuffings out of Scarecrow. Yikes!

Let me refer you once again to the box, the path, and the circus. While a typical circus lures us in with the smell of popcorn and clown-prompted laughter, at the end of the show you are free to go.

Not so for your circus of sexual obsession—especially at the level of addiction. Though willingly lured in by the promises of fulfilled fantasies, those freakish monkeys soon chain you to the bleachers, making escape seem impossible. Repeated failures to leave the big top are maddening.

How did those monkeys slip on the chains? How can they keep us so imprisoned?

While this lesson is not meant to be a thorough explanation of the latest science on sexual addiction, it will provide guidance on how to be ushered over the sawdust, out of the stuffy circus air, and into God's healing light.

Yeah, we are going to find out what feeds those darn monkeys.

Windows of Grace and Truth

Want to drive a struggling heroin addict crazy? Look them in the eyes and firmly state, "You ought to just quit! Just don't stick that needle in your arm! Just stop it!"

But I am guessing that you have said the same thing to yourself, over and over again. "Just don't go to that website! Delete their phone number from your cell! Get rid of the stash of videos!" It's not quite so easy, is it?

Everyone caught in a cycle of repeated sexual failure has some degree of genetic predisposition that makes them vulnerable. Then there are issues from our past that feed the addictive draw of the activity which tempts us.

Terry Wardle has pioneered a discipline of Christian counseling called formational prayer. His book *Healing Care, Healing Prayer* describes the dynamics of inner healing through what he calls the Structures of Healing. This paradigm so clearly ties together the wholeness and holiness our souls long for.

The Structures of Healing[1]

Life Situations

Dysfunctional Behaviors

Emotional Upheaval

Lies & Distortions

Wounds

At the top of this diagram you find Life Situations. A simpler term would be "Trouble"! Threats of divorce, financial collapse, loss of a job, and conflict with key people all sound an alarm that something is wrong. The monkeys' chains have you bound, but how did they get such power? Well, it's on the lower levels of these structures where you will find what feeds them. So let's look there to find their stash.

All of us experience emotional wounding during our lives. There are basically two general types of wounds. First, there are those things which have happened to us, such as abuse, betrayals, traumatic events, and shaming. The younger we are, the greater impact they can wield.

---

1. Terry Wardle, *Healing Care, Healing Prayer: Helping the Broken Find Wholeness in Christ* (Orange, CA: New Leaf Books, 2001), 137.

The other type of wounds are deprivations. Each of us are born with core longings. Things like love, security, understanding, purpose, significance, and belonging. Growing up in a home where some of these are lacking has an effect on us. And to some degree, we all have areas of neglect. All of us. And it is these unmet longings that make us so vulnerable to unhealthy behaviors.

What happens when we experience wounds of either type? It cracks open the shell of our soul a bit, and gives the Father of Lies a chance to plant a variety of lies, distorting our understanding of who we are, who God is, and what life is like.

And lies cause pain. Some folks march through life to a constant drumbeat: "You are disgusting! No one will ever want you! God doesn't love you! God could never forgive you! Sex is your greatest need!" Can you imagine how that would create inner pain and stress? Of course you can! Some of those very messages are pounding away in your own head.

So what do we do with the pain? Well, as the diagram illustrates, we adopt dysfunctional behaviors to kill the pain, to avoid further pain, or to fill the aching unmet need. And repeated use of sexual stimulation is your drug of choice.

Internet pornography is so highly addictive, nearly anyone can get hooked. But we all have wounds and lies that feed the monkeys that torment us. Finding healing for the wounds and lies of our past can provide a key toward starving these incessant monkeys and gaining victory.

Band Discussion Questions

- Does the circus metaphor work for you? In what ways does the pull of sexual temptation seem at all like being lured into a tent and chained to the bleachers?
- Does anything from the Structures of Healing ring true for you? In other words, can you make clear connections between the wounds of the past and your present-day obsessions?
- What lies do you think bounce around inside your head?

The Three Cs

Few things keep us chained to the bleachers as do our secrets. Confession is good for the soul when brought before people we trust and love. Yes, very good for the soul.

- **C**onfessing to One Another

  — What sexual sins have you committed since we last met?
  — What temptations did you face successfully?
  — How did you overcome those temptations?
  — Did you do anything questionable that you are not sure was sinful?

- **C**oaching One Another

  What made you vulnerable to temptation? Were you:

Hungry?

Angry?

Lonely?

Tired?

Stressed?

Bored?

- **C**leansing One Another

  What prayer keys would be helpful for you today?

Prayer Key: Lament (Part 1)

Okay, can I bring up an unpleasant subject? Trust me, this is eventually going to make sense, but I want to talk about *vomiting*.

We've all been there. Your stomach churns like a cement mixer. An achy feeling envelopes your body. Sweat beads up on your face as warm saliva begins to flow in your mouth. You know you will feel better if you can just hurl it out, but you hate doing it. The tortured tummy somehow seems preferable.

And let's face it. Vomiting is not only messy, it burns your throat, leaves chunks lodged in your nose, and it tastes *nothing* like the food that first entered your mouth. Yuck! And it can be a lonely—hugging a commode with water splashing onto your face. Ugh.

But whether you are forcing yourself to barf or it is coming up unbeckoned, you know within a few minutes you are going to feel much better.

As strange as it may seem, I believe there's a good bit of similarity between vomiting and how we handle our emotions. We've heard many times that it is not good to stuff your feelings. *Don't hold them in. You need to let them out.* But North Americans typically find this messy. Unpleasant. Embarrassing, really.

The moment one begins to cry in public, the first word out of someone else's mouth is usually, "Sorry!" Sorry for what? It's just that we have been conditioned to keep our sorrows and heartaches under wraps. So what do we do? We stuff. We know we will feel better if we can just hurl them out, but it is so messy!

This week and next we are going to learn about the biblical means of dealing with our emotions. The Bible was written in a culture that grieved openly, spilling their hearts out to one another and to God. David the giant-killer and king is our greatest example. The Psalms are pages ripped from his journal, revealing how he cried out to God with his emotions. It's not a North American thing to do, but it is absolutely biblical, no matter how messy it gets.

Whether you realize it or not, your soul has been churning over the ungrieved wounds of your past. Your drug of choice has been sexual release. But biblical lament is the good heave ho that lessens our pain and gives less for the circus monkeys to feed on.

While we will not use this prayer key today, the following assignment will move you in the direction of learning to lament.

Assignments

Read Lesson 7: "The Impact of Abuse."

Connect with your band of brothers (or sisters) daily.

Connect with God daily using "The Divine Office for Sexual Strugglers" as usual. But be sure that you read the following Psalms. Note the emotions that these writers express to God and try to answer the questions that follow.

Read Psalms 6, 13, 31, 51, 55, 73, and 142.

What seems to be the writer's problem?

What exactly is he feeling?

What does it say about his relationship with God?

Write a brief letter to God about a pocket of pain you've stuffed. Ask the Spirit to guide you to the right loss. It might be about what your obsession has cost you. Or perhaps it will be about how some form of abuse affected your life.

A Promise of Victory

A promise of victory gives us hope. But what does victory look like? Simply put, *abiding in Christ*. As you read in appendix B, knowing Christ through intimacy and obedience is the aim.

That's the thrust of this cycle. Victory is not the absence of struggle, but winning out over the struggle. The transformation God promises does include a lessening of bondage to sexual desire, but not the removal of all temptation. His first desire for us is to walk closely with him, and sometimes it is the very siren call of sexual pleasure that causes us to bind ourselves more tightly within his embrace.

To that end, move on to the third cycle of the divine office, keeping in mind that this disciplined practice of prayer and Scripture reading is not the medicine for what ails you. It simply binds your heart more tightly with the Doctor! It is his holy love that sets us free.

This cycle of lessons provides further insight as to what issues in our past fuel the maddening urges to grasp for what is not ours. You will also find greater attention given to the matter of addiction and how God does his healing work.

And at this point in your journey together as a band, perhaps it is fitting to address the frequency of slipups among you. The goal is ninety days. You are halfway there! But if someone in your group has collapsed nearly every week, it might be important to look for an outside resource to help with their recovery. Would sessions with someone trained in formational prayer be called for? Or time spent with a certified sex addiction therapist? The Come Away with Me retreats sponsored by Healing Care Ministries might also provide the turning point someone needs.

If you are the person slipping up week by week, you might find the insights in appendix B encouraging.

And consider this: How are frequent slipups affecting the will and resolve of others in the band? This could be a very helpful conversation to have.

The Impact of Abuse

Have you ever had a smoke alarm go off in the night? The ear-piercing screech awakens you with a jolt. You quickly yank out the battery and then, hopefully, you look for the source of the smoke. It would be insane to simply go back to bed. The alarm is the messenger! It tells you something is wrong somewhere in the house!

Pain and anxiety are alarms. They signal something is wrong somewhere in our soul. But if we keep killing the messenger with our addictive behaviors, we won't find the pain that needs God's healing grace.

Be assured that Satan wants you to remain numb. If you follow the messenger, you will discover the old lies and wounds that feed the monkeys.

But staying numb keeps us dumb. Instead of killing the pain, I urge you to take the pain to God with the prayer key of lament.

As you write letters to God, pour out the pain before him and receive his healing word.

Windows of Grace and Truth

In recent years, there has been a resounding cry of outrage as one victim of sexual abuse after another has told the world "Me too!" In many ways, this is a very good thing. Far too often the trauma of sexual abuse has been compounded by silencing victims, sweeping the dirt under the rug, and denying any type of just resolution.

Back in the 1990s, Patrick Carnes's research unearthed some startling statistics. Among sexual addicts, 81 percent had been sexually abused; 97 percent had been emotionally abused; 72 percent physically abused.[1] Wow! And the greatest ongoing fear for many was of being abandoned.

All abuse has an impact. But because our genitals are the closest outward connection to the deepest part of our being, unwanted touch and other sexual violations take the pain that much deeper into our hearts. If the abuser was someone we were close to, the pain of betrayal takes it deeper still. And if we reported it, and were told to keep quiet, shame and blame infect the wound mercilessly.

---

1. Patrick Carnes, *Sexual Anorexia: Overcoming Sexual Self-Hatred* (Center City, MN: Hazelden, 1997), loc. 190.

If abused as a small child, our trust in God can become shattered like the spider web cracks of a damaged windshield. We cry out, "Why would God allow this to happen to a little child? And, if he let this happen back then, how can I trust him to help me now?"

With such a shattered view of God, we are unable to look to the very one who is best able to help us. Maddening, right?

What does this abuse look like? Mic Hunter, in his excellent book *Abused Boys*, provides a comprehensive list of abusive activities, which involve far more than contact with genitals. Abuse includes having a child touch someone inappropriately, introducing pornographic materials to them, peeping in on them in the shower, exposing oneself to them, or simply using sexualized talk. In fact, even verbal sexual abuse can be as disturbing as sexual touch given the right circumstances.[2]

Reading that list of activities helps us see one reason why past abuse is denied. Our definition is not broad enough. Some simply don't view what happened to them as technically abusive.

How does abuse affect us? Carnes maintains that sexual abuse typically sends us in one of two directions: sexual addiction or sexual aversion. The impact can leave us craving for more, or avoiding intimacy of any kind.

---

2. Mic Hunter, *Abused Boys: The Neglected Victims of Sexual Abuse* (New York: Fawcett Columbine, 1990), 8–22.

And so it is very much worth your time to ask the Holy Spirit to reveal those issues of abuse that are in your past.

If a memory of abuse jumps out at you, it might possibly be an assignment from the Spirit to write a new lament and bring to your band. *Possibly.* However, if the band does not feel like a safe and proper place, find someone trained in dealing with sexual abuse or emotional trauma. A seasoned veteran of formational prayer might be a good choice, or someone certified in EMDR (Eye Movement Desensitization and Reprocessing).

Move in the direction of finding healing. If properly treated, you will be surprised how the pull toward sexual temptation will be lessened.

Band Discussion Questions

- As you read the list by Mic Hunter, were there any surprises?
- Did any memories of abuse surface as you prepared for today? What details are you able to share?
- Does the fear of abandonment resonate with you at all? Were there incidents in childhood that may have instilled a fear of losing a parent?
- Was your first sexual experience abusive? If so, do you ever find yourself trying to recreate that first experience through fantasy or foreplay?

The Three Cs

Confession can get tricky when it comes to sexual abuse. There is a deep and persistent lie that murmurs, "You know, you were not completely innocent. Somehow you wanted that touch." Why does this lie feel so very true? There are a number of possibilities, really.

Children are often groomed for the abuse. Predators give gifts, show attention, and lavish compliments as they are reeling their victims in. Hungry hearts take it all in like warm chocolate chip cookies, thinking someone finally loves and appreciates them.

Add to this the fact that when our genitals are touched, we are wired to bond. If the touch is gentle, it can be very pleasurable. This sends a confusing message for the abused.

Denial is almost a given when an older woman exploits a boy for sexual pleasure. His buddies will likely shout, "Wow, you got lucky!" But my experience as a counselor tells me all of the luck was bad. More often than not, such abuse sends the boy tailspinning into manhood, chasing one sexual high after another.

And so, take care to confess only what is yours to confess. Abuse victims are *victims*. Regardless of how it felt, you were not at fault.

- **C**onfessing to One Another

    — What sexual sins have you committed since we last met?
    — What temptations did you face successfully?

— How did you overcome those temptations?

— Did you do anything questionable that you are not sure was sinful?

• **C**oaching One Another

What made you vulnerable to temptation? Were you:

Hungry?
Angry?
Lonely?
Tired?
Stressed?
Bored?

• **C**leansing One Another

What prayer keys would be helpful for you today?

Prayer Key: Lament (Part 2)

Brace yourselves, oh squeamish ones. We're back to the subject of vomiting.

Just as upset stomachs find release when we retch and heave, so our souls find rest and peace as we pour out our emotions. But we just don't like the messy process.

Here's another key point. Whether emptying our stomachs or hurling out our emotions, there's the matter of finding the right location. Vomiting on people will not win you any friends. Neither will spewing out your anger into the faces of others! The proper target for expression, according to the Scriptures, is God himself.

As you read the psalms listed in your assignments for this week, you saw David and Asaph crying out to God with their anger, fear, and pain. And sometimes the anger was with God!

One can imagine David writing out Psalm 13 as a fugitive on the run for his life. "Hey, God, you said I was to be the next king! Where are you? Did you forget about me?"

And have you ever identified with Asaph in Psalm 73? "Hey, God, the corrupt fat cats are getting off scot-free! What about me? I'm doing all the right things and I keep getting the shaft!"

There are even hateful words that we would hesitate to say in front of our kids! Did you catch what David said about his buddies that betrayed him? "Let death come upon them; let them go down alive to Sheol" (Ps. 55:15). Basically, David cried out, "God, knock them into hell before they know what hit them!"

But the most important part of lament is this: meeting God. Hearing his voice. Getting a sense of his presence. And that is what we find in many of the Psalms.

Consider Psalm 6. We don't know the circumstances, but David is in emotional distress and physical agony. Fearing for his life, he is soaking his bed with tears. But at some point after writing verse 7, he encounters God.

Meeting God in the mess of our emotions keeps us from sliding into one of two extremes: a ceaseless cycle of wallowing, or stiff-upper-lip stuffing for life. Meeting God brings healing.

And the more healing we find for those stuffed pockets of inner pain, the less compulsion we will have to seek out our painkillers.

Assignments

Read Lesson 8: "Restoration and Grace."

Connect with your band of brothers (or sisters) daily.

Connect with God daily using "The Divine Office for Sexual Strugglers" as usual.

Write a brief letter to God about a pocket of pain you've stuffed. Ask the Spirit to guide you to the right loss. It might be about what your obsession with sex has cost you. Or perhaps it will be about how some form of abuse affected your life.

Restoration and Grace

You have been putting a lot of time, energy, and prayer into overcoming sexual struggles. While that is not the only monkey you have, it is the one currently screaming in your face. By God's grace and the work of the Holy Spirit, you are gaining control of that area of your life.

How can we cooperate with the Holy Spirit more fully? One way is to improve our ability to recognize his voice.

Today's prayer key is an exercise to help you improve your spiritual listening skills. God wants us all to be able to hear from him more clearly. The main reason to hear from God is simply to learn to love him more! But he will also use your spiritual ears to guide your healing process, and eventually to help others overcome monkeys of their own.

Windows of Grace and Truth

"Already and not yet." This phrase is a key to understanding the work of God at the present time. In some ways, the kingdom of God is already here in its fullness. Freedom and healing are available to some degree in this life. But the fullness of the kingdom will come when we see the King.

Can God heal sickness instantaneously? Absolutely. Perhaps you've witnessed that firsthand. And sometimes his healing is rapid and progressive, but not instantaneous. But there are other instances when we pray with seemingly no visible results. Just grace to endure. But one day we will step into the next life where all such sickness will be behind us.

"Already and not yet." It applies to this matter of sexual healing as well. Have I witnessed immediate healing for areas of sexual brokenness? Yes, but usually freedom comes in degrees. And some never find full freedom from temptation, but they are able, by God's sustaining grace, to endure the daily onslaught.

The arrival of Jesus Christ and his costly death on the cross secured the beachhead of the kingdom. From there, the kingdom has been advancing around the globe. Note how the apostle Paul described the taking of that beach:

Have this mind among yourselves, which is yours in Christ Jesus, who, though he was in the form of God, did not count equality with God a thing to be *grasped*, but *emptied* himself, by taking the form of a servant, being born in the likeness of men . . . he humbled himself by *becoming obedient* to the point of death. (Phil. 2:5–7, 8b ESV, italics added)

Remember the descriptions of puppy dogs and predators? Predators grasp for what is not theirs. Puppies, however, submit to this created world by leaning into people in inappropriate ways.

Note that in Philippians 2, Jesus modeled the way forward. He emptied himself instead of grasping. He humbled himself and submitted to the Father's plan, instead of submitting to the comforts of this world.

The starting point for overcoming any temptation is *submitting* to God. James 4 tells us, "Resist the devil, and he will flee from you." But the sentence right before it is, "Submit yourselves therefore to God" (v. 7). God's power for resisting Satan is released when we fully submit.

We may be fighting off hornets the rest of our lives. The pull of pornography may always be present. Unwanted online advances may continue. But God can enable us to resist consistently as we submit to him.

In Psalm 34:19, David reflects on his own adversities, affirming that we will always have struggles of one sort or another. "Many are the afflictions of the righteous." And yet despite his frequent disappointments, betrayals, and attacks, David assures us, "the LORD rescues them from them all."

Pray for the miracle for everyone in your band—that after these ninety days, you will all be able to brush off temptation with ease. But submit yourselves to God if the road is more difficult. Find his grace to pick up your cross daily and follow Jesus!

Band Discussion Questions

- Was there anything in this lesson that aggravated you?
- Was there an insight that you found helpful in your own struggle with sin?
- What makes it difficult for you when you think of having to bear this cross for the long term? Are you willing to take up that cross anyway?

The Three Cs

- **C**onfessing to One Another

    — What sexual sins have you committed since we last met?
    — What temptations did you face successfully?
    — How did you overcome those temptations?
    — Did you do anything questionable that you are not sure was sinful?

- **C**oaching One Another

    What made you vulnerable to temptation? Were you:

Hungry?
Angry?
Lonely?
Tired?
Stressed?
Bored?

- **C**leansing One Another

What prayer keys would be helpful for you today?

If someone has written a letter to God, here is how to help them process their lament:

- Begin with prayer, asking God to open up their heart so that the pain can come out.
- Have them read the letter to God, telling him what this loss has cost them, what it has made them believe about themselves, and what they are now feeling.
- Lay hands on them and tell them to ask God if he has anything to say to them.
- If he spoke a word or brought something to mind, pray for God to seal that message in their hearts.
- Anoint with oil, praying for God's healing of the pain.
- Lead them in the following prayer of renunciation: *God, thank you for hearing this prayer and sending your healing word. If any evil spirits had a foothold in my life as a result of that bottled-up pain, I command them to go in the name of Jesus. Fill me once again with your Holy Spirit. Amen!*

Prayer Key: Experiential (Safe Place) Prayer

Most believers agree that God does speak to us. Whether it is through reading Scripture, listening to a sermon, engaging in worship, or gazing at a starlit sky, we sense something in our spirits. Sometimes we actually hear his voice or see images.

What makes many uncomfortable with seeking to hear from God is they aren't quite sure that what they are experiencing is actually from him. It could simply be a word or image generated by one's busy mind. And then there's the influence of evil spirits. Perhaps the word or picture that popped into their mind was from an evil source.

With time, however, we can learn to distinguish his voice from the clutter of the mind. And experiential prayer is a way of positioning ourselves to maximize our discernment. The letters C-S-I can help you remember the process:

Centering through Praise: Have someone in the group lead you in a prayer of worship. This will center and quiet your minds as you focus upon the glory and gifts of God. This doesn't have to be a long prayer. Something as simple as the following will suffice:

> *Gracious God, we praise you as the one true God: Father, Son, and Holy Spirit. You have opened the way into your kingdom through the blood of Jesus Christ. Through the cross, we have access to cleansing, forgiveness, and healing. You are so good to us, your children.*

<u>Silencing</u> the Enemy: Having focused your minds by centering on God, then very simply silence the enemy with this prayer:

Through the cross, you have disarmed the enemy. And in the name of Jesus, if there are any evil spirits present, we command you to be silent. We bind you. You cannot interfere in any way.

<u>I</u>nviting the Holy Spirit: Ask the Holy Spirit to speak to you.

The only spirit we want to hear from is the Holy Spirit. So we invite you, Holy Spirit, to open our eyes and ears to see and hear all that you have to say to us.

When you have centered your soul through praise, have silenced the enemy, and have invited the Holy Spirit to speak, simply rest in silence. You might begin to have a feeling of peace or warmth. Perhaps you will hear a word or phrase. Some folks see flashes of light.

For many, a picture begins to form in their minds. Sometimes it is a place familiar to them, but often it is not. When such images are from God, they provide a sense of peace. If you see a safe place, ask God to meet you there. Soak in all that you see.

And regardless of what you see or don't see, ask God if he has a word for you. And when you sense you are done, write in the following space what you heard and saw.

Observations from Experiential Prayer:

Assignments

Read Lesson 9: "Where to Draw Lines."

Connect with your band of brothers (or sisters) daily.

Connect with God daily using "The Divine Office for Sexual Strugglers" as usual.

Practice 5–10 minutes of experiential prayer for three days. And no worries if you don't hear or see anything. Simply rest in God's presence as you would in centering prayer.

Where to Draw Lines

"As long as both parties are consenting adults and nobody gets hurt . . ." Have you heard that before? Yeah, probably you've acted on that before as well. Such thinking is not a remnant of the sexual revolution. It's a pickup line from the beginning of time.

One lady asked me where the Bible prohibited BDSM (Bondage, Dominance, Sado-Masochism). She had found being tied down and whipped while experiencing orgasm had brought a lot of peace to her. Seriously. She stated that she now felt more confidence and was more comfortable with her body image. Unlike other sexual experiences, when she said, "Stop, that hurts," the dominant partner would actually stop. Ironically, she felt safe and whole by submitting to whippings.

The Bible is certainly specific about a number of sexual behaviors, but BDSM isn't on the list. However, the garden of Eden, as described in Lesson 1, is our guide, regardless of whether there is consent and safety. Anything outside of the garden falls short. And the further we stray from lovemaking that is covenantal, consensual, loving, and relational, the more destructive it will be. Bank on it.

Windows of Grace and Truth

Fudging. Justifying. Rationalizing. We've all done it. In the heat of the moment with hormones and longings urging us forward, we have an amazing capacity to compromise.

And the dynamics of sexual temptations are confounding, aren't they? Resolutions are discarded and common sense seems paralyzed. We want what we want. *Period.* So we go for it . . . and almost immediately we experience regret.

Knowing that Scripture clearly outlines the boundaries of sexual expression is important to know long before we reach the heat of the moment. In this devolving culture of ours, we are inundated increasingly with the message that multiple means of sexual expression with multiple partners (imaginary or real) is absolutely fine—as long as nobody gets hurt.

People are calling the Old Testament laws into question, especially as same-sex marriage has been debated. Inevitably, someone says, "Hey, there are a lot of crazy laws in the Bible we don't follow anymore. We now eat pork and shellfish. And we don't make demands on types of fabric and farming practices. So why get so picky on the sexual laws?"

Such reasoning continues with, "If Jesus came to fulfill the law, and said to simply love God and our neighbors as ourselves, why not let people decide for themselves whom to love and how to make love?"

This debate is not quite so simple, and it calls us to understand the different types of laws in God's Word and why he gave laws to his people in the first place.

Long before the life and death of Jesus Christ secured the beachhead mentioned in the previous lesson, God softened up the beach by preparing a people. He chose Abraham, brought his descendants out of Egypt and through the Red Sea, and then began a centuries-long process of shaping their view of God and his ways.

Through the laws, God communicated that he is holy and he wants his people to be holy as well. Some laws were moral laws, drawing clear boundaries on right and wrong behavior. Laws such as murder, stealing, and adultery are wrong in any culture or at any time of history.

Other laws were civil in nature. They governed the life of Israel, laying out timeless principles and applying them to their life in that context. They gave direction on what it means to love neighbors in an ancient agrarian culture. Some of those laws are obsolete, but the principles are foundational for laws in any society.

However, there were laws that God gave them simply to teach them the concepts of holiness, sin, redemption, and atonement.

These were ceremonial laws. Like object lessons for kids, they pointed to higher truths, especially the coming of one who was the truth—the final sacrifice to fulfill all such laws.

Ceremonial laws included what one could eat, how one should dress, and when to plant crops. But Jesus declared all such laws fulfilled in him.

The sexual laws given to God's people were clearly moral in nature. The behaviors forbidden in Leviticus were given to warn God's people to not adopt the behaviors of their pagan neighbors. No, BDSM didn't make the list. Apparently, it wasn't a Canaanite thing. But all of the sexual laws given by God mirror the pattern in the garden of Eden.[1]

Don't allow Satan to use the sexual chaos of our culture to persuade you to compromise. God calls us to be his holy people, in the bedroom, in front of our computers, and on the cell phone screen. Let the garden be your guide.

God's sexual laws are not his way of squelching fun and frolic. They are not meant to inhibit sexual fulfillment and expressions of love. Instead, they point the way toward greater fulfillment and toward the truest expressions of love. It is in obeying God that ultimately nobody gets hurt.

---

1. For a more detailed explanation of the laws, see my book *Into the Light: Healing Sexuality in Today's Church* (Franklin, TN: Seedbed, 2016).

Band Discussion Questions

- Have you found the messages of our culture leading you into compromise?
- When we disobey God's sexual laws, who is getting hurt? Even with nameless pornography sites, there is a cost, isn't there?
- What harm has your sexual rebellion caused you? Your spouse? Or people you don't know?
- Did it bother you at all that the previous question used the word "rebellion"?

The Three Cs

- **C**onfessing to One Another

    — What sexual sins have you committed since we last met?

    — What temptations did you face successfully?

    — How did you overcome those temptations?

    — Did you do anything questionable that you are not sure was sinful?

- **C**oaching One Another

    What made you vulnerable to temptation? Were you:

    Hungry?
    Angry?

Lonely?
Tired?
Stressed?
Bored?

- **C**leansing One Another

What prayer keys would be helpful for you today?

Prayer Key: Renouncing Shame

Our culture is changing in many ways, sometimes at mind-numbing speed. And one *positive* change, I believe, is our growing awareness of the difference between guilt and shame.

Guilt is tied to behavior, while shame is linked with identity. Guilt hounds us because we've done something wrong. But the bite of shame is not about what we did as much as who we are. Shame says, "What kind of a person does something like that? What's wrong with you?"

Shame slimes us especially when our sins are sexual. To some degree, the church has contributed to this by avoiding sexual subjects and by making sexual sins seem more heinous than any other. And sexual sins, by nature, are deeply personal and thus bound up in identity issues.

And so it is, when we ask God to forgive us for acting out sexually, feelings of shame still cling to us even though we know we've been forgiven. There are deeply rooted lies that say that we are the grimy bathtub ring of the kingdom of God for having done such things.

There is a two-pronged approach to dealing with shame. The first prong is confessing our sins to a mature Christian who will not shame us. Confessing sins to God cleanses guilt. But as James 5:16 reminds us, it is in confessing our sins to another believer that we find healing. It lifts the shame off of us.

The second prong is an interaction with God. The truth from Scripture is that we are *far* from being the bathtub ring. We are dearly loved children who are seated in Christ Jesus.

But the voice of the enemy is deafening at times. So this prayer key involves trumping the enemy with the voice of the Spirit:

- Position yourself before God, using either centering or experiential prayer.
- Thank God for forgiveness of guilt.
- Renounce shame in Jesus' name.
- Ask God to speak the truth to you. In most cases, something immediately comes to mind: a word, a verse of Scripture, an image, or a song.
- Affirm the truth and renounce any spirits that had footholds because of shame.

Anytime you notice the slime of shame on the face of any band member, position them in the presence of Jesus and have them pray:

Thank you, God, that you have forgiven me for slipping back into my sinful behavior. I renounce shame in the name of Jesus. Gracious God, speak your truth into my soul.

Have them listen to see if he impresses something upon their soul. Then close with them praying:

Thank you, God, for this truth! I receive it in the name of Jesus. And if any evil spirits had a foothold in my life because of this shame, I command those spirits to go in Jesus' name! Amen!

Follow this by anointing them with oil and sealing the truth within them. A firm hug might help as well!

Assignments

Read Lesson 10: "The Elephant and the Scapegoat."

Connect with your band of brothers (or sisters) daily.

Connect with God daily using "The Divine Office for Sexual Strugglers" as usual.

For three days, practice 5–10 minutes of either experiential or centering prayer.

A Vision for the Church

Twelve-step programs and other recovery materials continue the healing journey by turning our vision outward. Similarly, this cycle begins the process of opening your eyes toward those who need help with issues of sexual brokenness.

If you have found significant victory over sexual temptation, and are well on your way toward your ninety days, perhaps now is a time to consider the church's need to offer similar ministry to others. This means addressing the contentious and divisive issues of sexual diversity and moving the church forward in a grace-filled and healing direction. This cycle addresses these concerns.

While our hope has been to see each band member cross the finish line, it is possible you are reading this as the sole survivor of your group. If that is the case, carefully select a pastor, colleague, or friend who can encourage you until you pass through the ninety-day window.

Note especially the final lesson. God has a purpose for your life. Being set free is enabling you to more fully know him and to complete his calling upon your life. Given the depth of sexual brokenness within our culture and the reluctance of most to address these issues, could it be God wants you to join the battle line? Consider how an equipped church can become the healing hands of Jesus!

The Elephant and the Scapegoat

've counseled people with sexual issues for many years. One thing I have sadly witnessed is self-hatred.

There are many reasons for this. Sometimes their behaviors have deeply wounded people they desperately love. Or labels have been slapped on their chests that seemingly won't go away. It could be the scarlet "A" for adultery. Some predators wear a muddy "M" for monster. And depending on one's attractions or fetishes, it could simply be a self-loathing for being beyond the norm.

Quite frankly, the church has been a culprit in prompting such self-hatred. We have piled on the shame by treating sexual sins as more sinful than any other disobedience. Just ask the average pew warmers what sin David committed. I'll bet anything, most will spit out the answer, "adultery!" Yeah, he did. But what about the murder? And denial? And arrogance? Why is the sexual sin the go-to answer?

Other than saying no, the church has been deafeningly silent on all matters sexual. Well, almost. Evangelicals have shouted from the rooftops that we believe same-sex behavior is sinful. And so I have observed a profound self-loathing among Christians who are attracted to the same sex.

All sin is equally sinful in the eyes of a holy God. And there are sinful behaviors in every box type of church. Judgmentalism, racism, materialism . . . just ask the unchurched. To them, hypocrisy in the church is as obvious and predictable as missing teeth on a hockey team.

Windows of Grace and Truth

Did you by chance grow up in the home of an alcoholic? There are certain dynamics that are typical of such a family. And, believe it or not, the same dynamics have played out in the church for generations. Let me explain.

If Dad is the drinker, Mom is usually the enabler. She rescues him by calling the boss in the morning, claiming her hubby is sick. She distracts the kids from the daily chaos. And if finances plummet, she may end up getting a job to make up for his lapses. If anyone brings up his drinking, the topic is soon swept under the rug.

The kids usually adopt certain roles in the midst of such a mess. The oldest becomes a parent of sorts, taking on chores and looking after the younger siblings. The youngest often takes to hiding, escaping into video games, TV, or novels.

Then there's the middle child, often known as the *scapegoat*. Hungering for any kind of attention, he or she wanders into trouble with tantrums, failed grades, fights, and sometimes problems with the law. At that point, all of the anger and anxiety within the family system gets aimed at this rebellious kid.

The next step is usually therapy. Both the parents and the oldest sibling are fuming, demanding that the caregiver fix this errant one. But if the counselor is wise, she or he will readily see that the main problem is not the kid at all. The real *elephant in the room* is the alcoholic dad.

This scenario has played out in the family of the American church. We have aimed our anger and angst at the scapegoat: the LGBT community. We've raised a ruckus over every advancement in gay rights, making this one issue the litmus test for any Christian leader. Gays and lesbians have been the scapegoat child for more than fifty years.

The elephant in the room? The pervasive problem no one has wanted to confront or address? It is the rampant sexual brokenness among heterosexuals within the pews. Few are brave enough to address it. It has been so much easier to aim our anger elsewhere.

Most studies reveal that at least one-third of all women and one-fifth of all men have been sexually abused. Thankfully, most churches are screening volunteers who work with children, but precious little has been done to address the hearts of those already broken by unwanted touch.

The rates of pornography addiction within stained-glassed sanctuaries doesn't fall far behind that of the unchurched world—and rates continue to rise.[1] Yet what have churches done to address this other than to shame people into accountability groups?

The elephant in the room is rarely mentioned. Any frank teaching on God's design for sexuality is swept and kept under the rug, unless it's pulled out for condemning people. It is assumed that sexual sin is out there and is somehow worse than any other sin.

But the scapegoat? It's been all the rage and an object of rage. Until recent years, the LGBT community had been addressed in piñata fashion, with evangelicals first in line to give it a whack.

Think I'm overexaggerating? One study published in 2007 found that the number-one reason millennials avoid church is they perceive Christians hate gays and lesbians.[2]

By the end of this book, I hope you will catch a vision for what the church can become when it comes to all forms of sexual brokenness. Church ought to be the safest place on earth to find healing for the sexual issues that plague us.

---

1. *The Porn Phenomenon: The Impact of Pornography in the Digital Age.* A Barna Report Produced in Partnership with Josh McDowell Ministry (a Cru Ministry), 2016, 13.

2. David Kinnaman and Gabe Lyons, *unChristian: What a New Generation Really Thinks about Christianity . . . and Why It Matters* (Grand Rapids, MI: Baker Books, 2007), 92.

But for now, simply consider how this elephant/scapegoat dynamic and the shameful stigmas that we've attached to sexual sins have affected your own battles with sexual temptation.

Band Discussion Questions

- Tell us about a time when you felt the elephant in the room was addressed well by God's people. Was it in a sermon? A Sunday school class? Small group?
- This lesson refers to the church shaming people into accountability groups. Has that been your experience? In fact, did you feel shamed into joining this group?
- Do you know of a person attracted to the same sex who feels shunned or shamed by the church?
- To what degree have you treated homosexual behavior as worse than heterosexual sin? Can you give examples?

The Three Cs

- **C**onfessing to One Another

    — What sexual sins have you committed since we last met?

    — What temptations did you face successfully?

    — How did you overcome those temptations?

    — Did you do anything questionable that you are not sure was sinful?

- **C**oaching One Another

  What made you vulnerable to temptation? Were you:

  Hungry?
  Angry?
  Lonely?
  Tired?
  Stressed?
  Bored?

- **C**leansing One Another

  What prayer keys would be helpful for you today?

Prayer Key: Renouncing Misogyny and Misandry

Since the day God announced Eve's offspring would crush the head of Satan, one hideous sin has permeated history: misogyny—the hatred and mistreatment of women. In a variety of ways, he has promoted the oppression of women.

Today's sex-trafficking is only a snowflake on the tip of the iceberg. Throughout the centuries, women have been forced to marry, forced into sexual practices, and treated as though they were mere property. In some countries today, babies are aborted simply for not being boys.

Men are often clueless. We have little idea how deeply women have been impacted by a culture that gives big-busted Barbies to little girls and holds up standards of body shape and beauty that so few can reach. Clueless.

Unequal pay is another example of misogyny. The only place women are guaranteed much higher pay? The pornography industry. There girls are paid to pretend they enjoy pain and humiliation. Their rate of pay for sex? Oral: $300. Anal: $1,000. Gangbang with three men: $1,300. No wonder the average female porn star career averages between six to eighteen months. They can't survive much longer.[3]

For the female bands using this material, likely you angrily resonate with these observations. Is it possible you hate yourself for being a woman? Or, perhaps you hold great hatred toward men.

Whether it is misogyny or misandry (hatred of men), we must repent. God has made us male and female in his image. By his design, we are his delight.

Each one in the band should pray this prayer wholeheartedly for any level of sin in hating people of a particular gender.

With each act of creation, O Lord, you proclaimed that this world is good. *And after creating man and woman, you said the world was* very good. *Forgive me for any hatred I have in my heart for myself and my own gender. Forgive also any and all hatred I have expressed, promoted, or participated in toward any gender.*

---

3. Maggie Jones, "What Teenagers Are Learning from Online Porn," *New York Times*, Feb. 7, 2018.

I renounce the lie that women are less valuable than men. I renounce the practice of viewing women or men as objects for my arousal. And I repent from any involvement in the industries that promote the mistreatment of women or men.

Satan has hated women from the beginning, and has sought to cheapen sex to no more than an act of idolatry, debasement, and oppression. If he has had a foothold in my life as a result of my misogyny, misandry, or hatred of myself, I command him to flee in the name of Jesus. Amen!

Assignments

Read Lesson 11: "Making Church a Sanctuary."

Connect with your band of brothers (or sisters) daily.

Connect with God daily using "The Divine Office for Sexual Strugglers" as usual.

For three days, practice 5–10 minutes of either experiential or centering prayer.

Making Church a Sanctuary

A sanctuary is not only a place to meet God, but an atmosphere that feels safe. And as you are gaining a vision for the church becoming the healing hands of Jesus, you may need some hazmat training. Yes, every church has hazardous material, and you need to be able to spot it and intervene in grace-filled ways.

Of all toxins, judgmentalism is the deadliest. We looked at that in Lesson 4 when we considered the box, the path, and the circus. Nothing sends sexually broken people out the door faster than the snooty glance of the fault-finding know-it-all. My guess is you can smell that corrosive crud from the parking lot.

But you may be smudged with some hazmat and not even notice it. Judgmentalism may not be the issue for you, but like some sexual strugglers, you may have a set of behaviors that keep your church less than welcoming.

Windows of Grace and Truth

My church is filled with recovering alcoholics and addicts. Some bring a lot of baggage with them. It can get messy. Sometimes it doesn't feel safe.

It's the only church where I've had to announce from the pulpit, "You can come to church high, but if you are selling drugs to people in our church, you are not welcome here!" And once I had to kick out a *member* of the church for obscene comments and inappropriate touch. I know. Weird.

One person simply has mannerisms and habits that are difficult to embrace. In fact, his actual embrace turns people off. His hugs resemble those of a professional wrestler. Ugh! He desperately needs friends, but unknowingly irritates the very people he so longs to befriend. It would help his cause greatly if someone would come alongside him and gently show him a better way.

Sexual addicts sometimes bring invisible baggage of their own. Will you allow me and the members of your band to come alongside you? Learning of the hazardous materials in your blind spot might help you see it in others.

Here's what I have observed:

Language

At one of the retreats where I serve as a counselor, one participant shouted out lightheartedly to the others, "Anyone else here part of the Mile High Club like I am?"[1] A deadening silence fell on the group, some of whom were victims of sexual abuse.

Often those obsessed with sex simply have poor filters. They use language that is inappropriate and sometimes downright offensive. Sexual innuendo, off-color wise cracks, and misogynistic slurs slide off their lips, and they aren't even aware of it!

Clothing

This is a tricky one. I get that. The latest fashions reflect our sex-soaked culture, and what seems inappropriate to one Christian is simply looking sharp to another. But there is a subtle message sent by the way we dress. Sexual addicts can push the boundaries too far without realizing it.

Simply put, there are ways of dressing that grab the attention of the opposite sex. We crave that attention, don't we? Cleavage for the woman or the unbuttoned shirt for the man grabs attention. Slits in jeans in suggestive spots scream out, "Hey, I'm naked under my clothes!" And it is empowering for many when their way of dressing turns heads and attracts flirtation.

No, there is no spiritual virtue in dressing sloppy. Looking ugly is not a fruit of the Spirit. But good boundaries include being conscious of what we wear. Dress nicely, even fashionably, but

---

1. Okay, you probably already know this, but the Mile High Club is made up of those who have had intercourse on an airplane at its highest altitude.

strive for good taste. Otherwise, you risk offending others and attracting toxic relationships.

Touching

When I bring up the subject of the five love languages to a sexual addict, they often say, "I think my love language might be touch." It seems that way. They long for skin-to-skin contact. Hugs are more than welcomed—they are craved!

And so some of us with sexual struggles can be far too touchy-feely and, once again, blind to it. Other folks cringe or politely keep some distance. Just as inappropriate dress can attract attention from unhealthy people, poor boundaries with physical affection can be a magnet for needy souls. Your hug lasts a good bit too long, and they just soak it up. And, quite honestly, you get the positive vibe from it too.

Yes, I get it. Good boundaries doesn't mean joining the Prickly Pear Fellowship. But being aware of these issues will promote healthier relationships.

Our deepest longing? Connection. Our dysfunctional way of meeting that need has been sexual consumption. But we can make it easier to receive the loving connection we need from healthy relationships if we give attention to our boundary issues. In the process, we make church a sanctuary where people can find the healing of our Savior.

The following questions are meant to help us find our blind spots. You will find them most helpful if you are most truthful!

Band Discussion Questions

- In the past, have you personally worked on the boundary issues of language, clothing, and touching?
- Are you willing to hear what others in the band have noticed about your boundaries in these three areas?
- If everyone is willing to be open and honest, what have you noticed in your interactions with each other?
- Have any of your band members shown inappropriateness in how they talk about sexual issues? If so, how could they have spoken differently?
- Has anyone seemed to be overly revealing in the way they dress? Be specific.
- If you've had opportunity to observe this, how does each member handle issues of physical affection?
- If you were called on your speech, attire, or touch, how did that make you feel? And do you believe it is something that should be changed?

The goal is not snobbishness, but to have good friendships with healthy people. We want church to be a safe and shame-free zone for those who struggle.

The Three Cs

- **C**onfessing to One Another

    — What sexual sins have you committed since we last met?
    — What temptations did you face successfully?
    — How did you overcome those temptations?
    — Did you do anything questionable that you are not sure was sinful?

- **C**oaching One Another

    What made you vulnerable to temptation? Were you:

    Hungry?
    Angry?
    Lonely?
    Tired?
    Stressed?
    Bored?

- **C**leansing One Another

    What prayer keys would be helpful for you today?

Prayer Key: Re-Imprinting

It seems we are wired in such a way that our very first sexual experience has an imprinting effect upon us. Ideally, our first sexual experience takes place within the security of a marriage covenant at a time when you and your spouse are head over heels for each other. If so, then the imprint from such an experience should be very positive and affirming.

Sadly, for most of us, that was not the setting for our first sexual encounter. If your first initiation was abuse, you likely view sex as something done *to* you instead of *with* you. Or perhaps your first experience was in the backseat of your dad's car. Your buddies may have coached you in just the right things to say and do so that you could get what you wanted. The resulting imprint? You view your spouse as the reluctant partner who must be manipulated to meet your needs.

One's imprint can seem nearly indelible. Is there no way to undo the damage?

Over the years, God has given me a simple way to position people before the Lord to re-imprint our sexual template. Think of the imprint as an old-fashioned wax seal on the back of an envelope. How do you change the seal without breaking it to pieces? By heating it up, of course, and stamping it with a new seal.

With this prayer key, we ask the Holy Spirit to, in essence, heat up the old imprint that has been sealed with an unholy experience. Then we ask God to bring to mind a memory or an image of sexual intimacy that most closely conforms to his good and loving design. This can be accomplished with the following steps with a band member leading another as follows:

- Position the person in centering prayer. Let them simply bask in the presence of God for a few minutes.
- Ask if you can lay hands on them.
- Ask the Lord to bring to their minds a memory or an image that represents for them his design for sexuality.
- When they see a memory or image in line with God's design, anoint their forehead and pray, *Lord Jesus, seal this as the new imprint upon [his/her] soul.*
- Have them repeat after you the following prayer of renunciation: *In Jesus' name, I renounce the old imprint and any level of demonization which came with it. Lord, I affirm this new imprint which reflects your truth. Amen.*
- Close with a prayer of thanksgiving.

Remind them to keep this image or memory in mind each time they are tempted to go back to the old way of thinking about sexual intimacy.

Assignments

Read Lesson 12: "The Importance of Welcoming the Wilde."

Connect with your band of brothers (or sisters) daily.

Connect with God daily using "The Divine Office for Sexual Strugglers" as usual.

For three days, practice 5–10 minutes of either experiential or centering prayer.

The Importance of Welcoming the Wilde

Those familiar with English literature will recognize the name Oscar Wilde. As a poet, playwright, and promoter of the arts, he was a rising star among the well-to-do. The play "The Importance of Being Earnest" brought applause from the London elite, making him the J. J. Abrams of the late 1800s.

And, he also had a reputation for sexual excess—a reputation he well deserved.

His life mirrored, to some degree, the excesses found in the early pages of the Bible book of Ecclesiastes. Wealthy, attractive, flamboyant, and brilliant, he withheld nothing from himself that might bring sensual pleasure. There were no limits to his excesses. Even though married and the father of two, he had numerous affairs, especially with young men, at a time when sodomy was a criminal offense.

One of his young lovers was extremely obsessed with Wilde. At first, the obsession was mutual, playing out in lengthy love letters, luxurious weekend flings, and expensive trips to Europe. When Wilde attempted to end the relationship, the young man's obsession became maniacal. He stalked Wilde incessantly.

Eventually, however, the man's father pressed sodomy charges against Wilde, providing the love letters in court as evidence. It was a scandal that shook the literary world. But more to the point, it turned Wilde's world upside down.

During his two years in prison, he lost everything. His wife divorced him. Worse yet, the courts forbid Wilde contact with his two sons. His mother, the dearest person to him on earth, passed away, greatly distressed over the shame Wilde had brought upon the family. His considerable fortune was stripped away, including an extensive collection of famous paintings. And his most humiliating moment was being placed in stocks at the London train station where people laughed at him and mocked him.

While in the depths of anguish and despair, God met him powerfully in his prison cell. He secured a Greek New Testament, and began to meditate daily upon the life of Jesus. A radiance and exhilarating freedom began to take over his life. And immediately upon his release from prison, he sought spiritual help from the priests.

But because of the sodomy, *they refused to help.* They rejected him.

His friends stated that they never saw him weep so fiercely as when the church rejected him.

Windows of Grace and Truth

In his prison epistle *De Profundis*, Wilde points to the anguish and deprivation of his jail cell as the "holy ground" upon which he met Jesus Christ. He who had been obsessed with literary and artistic beauty became enthralled with the beauty of Jesus. Wilde fell at the feet of this one who embraced the greatest suffering *of all*, thus making Calvary the holiest ground *for all*.

And yet for Wilde, the church, the bride of this same Jesus, proved ugly. And it may be that your local church isn't much better looking.

Are you curious about the Latin title *De Profundis*? It means "out of the depths," and is taken from the first four words of Psalm 130, a psalm of repentance. Like the psalmist, Wilde came out of the depths of the consequences of his sin and into the embrace of God.

You no doubt have endured your own holy ground. Whether it has been suffering in the prison cell of consequences, or the stress of staying clean for these ninety days, suffering can move us out of the depths and into God's embrace.

Perhaps now is the point in your journey to look outward toward others who are experiencing their own holy ground. How desperately they need your church to be welcoming, kind, and nurturing. And yet, we've all experienced how ugly and judgmental the church can be, especially when it comes to sexual sin.

You and I can't say that we love Jesus the Bridegroom if we despise the bride. In fact, *you are part of the bride!* And as one who has come out of your own depths, you can have a part in being the welcoming arms of the church for others.

Some of you have learned how to spot a person in a park, rest stop, or elsewhere who is willing to hook up. There's a certain look you notice. And, in fact, I know of addicts so deep in the jungle of addiction that evil spirits actually lead them to willing partners. Perhaps that was you.

But now it is time for you to use those same eyes to spot the troubled person who walks into your fellowship. And instead of being led by evil spirits, you can be led by the Holy Spirit to reach out to searching people who need freedom from sexual sin and a deeper connection with the Savior.

It may be someone who hides it well. Or perhaps you see the weariness of the circus in the lines on their face. Whether your church is contemporary or traditional, high church or low church, you can become the welcoming arms for those walking out of their depths and through the doors of your church. Keep your eyes open.

Your church becomes a sanctuary also if people become comfortable talking in biblical ways about sexuality. The pastor needs to set the tone, so encourage her or him to address it often from the pulpit. People hear the world's message about sex from just about every venue. Why not hear God's message on Sunday mornings?

There are many resources available now for the savvy pastor or small-group leader. Let me suggest my own book *Into the Light*, which can be read privately or used in groups. And, certainly, you could encourage the formation of other bands. In fact, if you were able to reach ninety days, lead a group yourself!

And, finally, have some courage and find ways to share your testimony. Yes, it will be risky. There's no question someone might take offense. But it can be done tastefully and well. Describe your own journey out of the depths and into God's healing light.

Band Discussion Questions

- How welcoming and judgment-free did your church feel before people knew about your sexual failures? What about after people found out?
- What would make your church seem safer and more welcoming for people who are known strugglers with sex or pornography?
- What part could you see yourself playing in moving people toward this vision of the church?

The Three Cs

- **C**onfessing to One Another

    — What sexual sins have you committed since we last met?

    — What temptations did you face successfully?

    — How did you overcome those temptations?

    — Did you do anything questionable that you are not sure was sinful?

- **C**oaching One Another

    What made you vulnerable to temptation? Were you:

    Hungry?
    Angry?
    Lonely?
    Tired?
    Stressed?
    Bored?

- **C**leansing One Another

    What prayer keys would be helpful for you today?

Prayer Key: Renunciation of Baal and Ashtoreth

In chapter 5 of my book *Into the Light*, I describe how worship of the ancient god Baal evolved into sexual orgy. It was the altar of Baal that Gideon was instructed to tear down before accepting his call as commander of Israel's forces. Because the worship of Baal and the fertility goddess Ashtoreth exemplified what it meant to put sex at the center of the universe, renouncing them was Gideon's first step.

In her ministry to people with great sexual brokenness, Leanne Payne found the healing path forward often included a renunciation of Baal and Ashtoreth. And in my own counseling practice, there are times when I feel prompted by the Spirit to have people renounce Baal and Ashtoreth, especially if they have been involved in great perversity. For many, this renunciation is a liberating moment.

In this cycle of lessons, we are piecing together a vision for what the church can become. Could it be God is calling you to prepare for a ministry to others caught up in sexual idolatry? Your first step is the same as it was for Gideon: renouncing Baal.

One by one, have members of your band pray this prayer before God:

Thank you, Lord God Almighty, for forgiving me of my sexual sins. Thank you for the healing that I've been experiencing in these weeks. And if my sinful behaviors have aligned me in any way with Baal and Ashtoreth, I now renounce them in the name above all other names, the name of Jesus! And if any evil spirits have had footholds in my life as a result of this alignment, I command them to go in Jesus' name. Amen.

Assignments

Read Lesson 13: "When Will This Ever End?"

Connect with your band of brothers (or sisters) daily.

Connect with God daily using "The Divine Office for Sexual Strugglers" as usual.

For three days, practice 5–10 minutes of either experiential or centering prayer.

When Will This Ever End?

Late one evening I received a desperate phone call. Clara was in trauma and could barely choke out the words: "Pastor, please come!"

Clara began attending our church because we were recovery friendly and she was an alcoholic. But soon she was receiving counseling for sexual abuse that had begun in early childhood and followed her throughout life. She had been like a magnet for predators. In fact, her second husband had courted her so that he could sexually dominate her and prey upon her two children.

Soon I and a lady from the church arrived. As we comforted this precious, weeping woman, she told us of a phone call from her daughter in Texas. Clara's grandson was in the ICU after having been seduced by a neighbor, taken out into the woods, violently raped, shot, and left for dead. This violation tapped into all the remaining rage for the injustices committed against her.

As we wrapped our arms around her and prayed for the presence of Jesus to descend, she finally she blurted out, "When will this ever end? It just keeps on happening. First my mother was abused, then me, then my kids, and now my grandson! Oh God!"

Her question still haunts me. When *will* incest, rape, sextrafficking, hookups, abuse, and sexual addiction finally come to an end? When will the sins of our ancestors cease to cycle through succeeding generations? Ultimately, not until Jesus returns. But in the meantime, we can seek his enabling to break the chains of abuse and sexual idolatry in our own families, and equip our churches to be the healing hands of Jesus.

Windows of Grace and Truth

In previous lessons, I have referenced Patrick Carnes, the pioneer in the research and treatment of sexual addiction. Having begun his work in the early 1980s, he has retired in recent years. In one of his last lectures, he made the startling statement that a sexual tsunami would hit our shores in the coming years.[1] Why?

Not so long ago, parents began giving iPads and other devices to small kids as babysitters. With young children's brains being immature, their neuropathways are now being shaped in ways

---

1. "Dr. Patrick Carnes' Last Lecture Pt. 1," delivered at Pine Grove Behavioral Services and Forrest General Hospital, https://www.you tube.com/watch?v=IwFc4GxtVJ0.

never seen before in history. The risk-and-reward nature of video games are rewiring malleable young minds in addictive directions. They will be far more prone toward addictions of all sorts.

Add to this the horrifying stat mentioned earlier that a child's first exposure to pornography is on average age eleven. Yes, *that's the average.* Carnes predicted addiction to Internet pornography would go through the roof. And given the distorted way in which sex is portrayed, abuse and misogyny will be caught up in the raging wave.

As of this writing, that was seven years ago, and already we see the crest of the wave about to slam the shores of our country. So what can we do?

Tsunamis are deadly. They give little warning. The one that slammed Japan in 2011 took 18,000 lives and exacted $285 billion from that island nation.

While it is difficult to prepare for such a disaster, we can certainly be involved in the relief effort for this current tsunami. Lessons 11 and 12 provided practical ways to move the church toward being a safe sanctuary for the broken. But now let's briefly consider ways you can be more deeply involved.

First of all, begin at home. If you have kids, don't wait until they reach puberty to have the talk. It needs to be an ongoing conversation beginning in their earliest years of development. And there are age-appropriate resources available to help.

Secondly, make it a matter of deep prayer. God may have some very specific ministries for you to embrace that line up with your gifts and passions. Perhaps you can teach in some capacity in your church, receive training in formational prayer to assist with healing, or oversee a ministry of bands using this material.

Finally, and most importantly, stay on the path. God's greatest desire for you is to experience more of him and his love. Grow in your intimacy with him. And as you walk in step with the Savior, your own personal healing will deepen.

Saint Bernard of Clairvaux advised his mentees to be reservoirs, not canals.[2] Receive deeply from the well of his grace so that what pours out upon others is an overflow of living water. Such a supply of his presence in your life will nourish and strengthen you and be a life-giving source for others.

Band Discussion Questions

- Reflect a bit. How has the study of this book affected you? And how has banding together been helpful?
- Which prayer key has been most liberating in the past three months?
- How do you personally intend to play a part in attacking the elephant of sexual brokenness in your life, church, and community?

---

2. Nicole Massie Martin, "Don't Give Away What's Meant for You: Can we find oxygen for exhausted souls in Song of Songs, of all books?" in CT Pastors Special Edition, "9 Time-Tested Mantras for Ministry," *Christianity Today* (2020): 31.

The Three Cs

- **C**onfessing to One Another

    — What sexual sins have you committed since we last met?

    — What temptations did you face successfully?

    — How did you overcome those temptations?

    — Did you do anything questionable that you are not sure was sinful?

- **C**oaching One Another

    What made you vulnerable to temptation? Were you:

    Hungry?
    Angry?
    Lonely?
    Tired?
    Stressed?
    Bored?

- **C**leansing One Another

    What prayer keys would be helpful for you today?

Prayer Key: Breaking Generational Cycles

Similar to Clara's story, you might be able to look back and see a pattern of sexual idolatry in your own family line. This is often a learned behavior. In fact, in the Old Testament you find lying to be passed on from Abraham to Isaac to Jacob and onward. The same with the sexual sins of David and his descendants. And yet, this is more than simply learned. There is a spiritual dynamic fueled by the work of evil spirits.

A colleague of mine once made an astounding claim: "I've had men expose themselves to me eight different times! And the strange thing is that my grandfather was put in prison for exposing himself to little girls." I assured her that this was more than a coincidence. The sins of her grandfather had opened up some vulnerability in the family line, and she had become a target. These men who exposed themselves were nudged by spirits to do so.

Prayers to break generational sins are not uncommon. Some are very lengthy and specific to certain sins or cultic involvements. But I have shaped the following prayer, informing it with content from Psalm 16.

Each one in your band should pray this prayer out loud. But before doing so, have someone read Psalm 16 so that you become familiar with its flow and content.

Lord Jesus Christ,

Protect me, Lord Jesus Christ, for I take refuge in you. You are my Lord, and every good thing I have comes from you.

Thank you for the elements of my heritage that have been good. Thank you for the boundary lines that have fallen for me in pleasant places. I embrace all the good that I have received from my ancestors, especially the holy ones.

I believe that "those who choose another god multiply their sorrows." And some of my ancestors have been involved in costly sins that have affected my generation. I know of _____ (name any sins that you know of from your ancestry). And no doubt there are unknown sins that have affected us as well.

In the name of Jesus, I break the effects of those sinful behaviors upon my generation and all succeeding generations. I also break the effects of my own sexual sins. May none of these sins cause my children to stumble.

To whatever degree evil spirits have made us vulnerable, I break their assignments over us in the name of Jesus and command them to flee.

You show me the path of life. Truly there is fullness of joy in your presence. As we keep you ever before us, may we not be shaken. May my generation and our descendants experience that joy, and may we together enjoy your pleasures in heaven forevermore. Amen!

Future Assignments

Has your band decided to disband or are you going to continue to urge each other onward? If you are sticking together in order to each reach your ninety days, here are some options.

First, check out Seedbed's website for information on bands. There are several options available, including the Daily Text, which is a devotional written by J. D. Walt and sent out daily via text message or e-mail. Each one in your band can join with a special format that allows you to see each other's comments as you reflect on the texts together.

In the future, a similar format will feature forty days' worth of devotionals on sexual temptation. Thus, you can stay together as a band and continue to interact daily online over material similar to what you've been processing these ninety days.

Finally, there are other excellent books written about sexual struggles which would work well for your group. One which I highly recommend is Michael John Cusick's *Surfing for God: Discovering the Divine Desire Beneath Sexual Struggle.*

Whatever course of action you take, be vigilant. Keep both feet on the path, making progress in your sexual holiness. And if necessary, seek counseling from qualified sources.

As each of us remain faithful in this ministry to the sexually broken, then perhaps fewer and fewer will cry out in despair, "When will this ever end?"

Appendixes

Some Thoughts on Masturbation

There is much difference of opinion among Christian teachers and psychologists about masturbation. One psychology teacher from a Christian college told me he believed it was God's gift to single people. On the other extreme, Ken Dyck of Freedom Session believes the practice is highly addictive and can never be practiced by a Christian. In his belief, God has given single men a natural way to release built-up semen as they sleep. Therefore, men will learn self-control and gain self-respect if they abstain totally from masturbation.

Between these two extremes are several variations. It is important, I maintain, that each one honestly hold this matter before the Lord and develop their own conviction. And so I simply offer the following observations.

The starting point is always Scripture. But what does the Bible say? Nothing, specifically. Of all the many sexual sins listed in the

Old Testament, this is not one of them. But there are certainly scriptural principles upon which to build your convictions.

Jesus was very clear about lust. In the Sermon on the Mount, he said, "everyone who looks at a woman with lust has already committed adultery with her in his heart" (Matt. 5:28). Note that the sin is not simply looking, but looking lustfully—making her an object of idolatrous longing.

Therefore, playing out sexual scenes in one's mind with a person other than one's spouse is a sin. This, quite obviously, rules out the use of pornography for sexual stimulation.

Some believe the next two verses refer to the actual act of masturbation:

> "If your right eye causes you to sin, tear it out and throw it away; it is better for you to lose one of your members than for your whole body to be thrown into hell. And if your right hand causes you to sin, cut it off and throw it away; it is better for you to lose one of your members than for your whole body to go into hell."
> (Matt. 5:29–30)

Clearly adultery is more than hopping in the sack with someone. As I have pointed out in Lesson 5, there is a bonding process with another that begins with a look of lustful longing. What becomes adulterated is the bond with our spouse. This bond is further polluted when you add masturbation to the mix.

But could it be that masturbating while thinking of one's spouse is permitted? There are certainly times when health, distance, or other factors make sexual intimacy impossible.

Additionally, consider the Scriptures' encouragement for sexual intimacy in marriage. To the sex-crazed city of Corinth, the apostle Paul urged wives and husbands to not withhold sex from their partners so that they would each be less likely to fall to sexual temptation (see 1 Corinthians 7). Clearly, withholding from one's spouse is sin. If we are masturbating as a way of avoiding intimacy with our spouse, that is wrong. And so, by implication, we can state that if you are masturbating as a way of withholding from your spouse or avoiding an issue in the relationship, this is clearly wrong.

Allow me to add some other considerations, which I've gleaned from my studies and my observations in working with people with sexual issues.

God designed us as sexual beings so that we can be more deeply connected with another person. Men have a buildup of semen which beckons for release about once every seven days. We are the only created beings who share sex in private and for emotional intimacy. And so it seems God has designed men to seek intimacy once a week.

One Jewish teacher stated that this falls in line with couples who incorporate lovemaking in their celebration of the Sabbath. Could it be God has so wired men to seek this Sabbath rest weekly?

Nocturnal emissions, it is said, occur about once every 7–28 days. And so some believe single men should simply wait until this happens. But what about those men for whom wet dreams are rare? I have known some to go more than fifty days without an emission, causing one man to carry around a donut cushion to ease his pain while sitting. Is it really God's will for that man to live with daily pain?

The most difficult situation is for the single person, especially men. If the need for release occurs for men every seven days, and nocturnal emissions are rare, does God truly call men to carry a donut cushion to ease the pain? And in light of Paul's word to the Corinthian married couples regarding a defense against sexual temptation, would God call upon single men to subject themselves to extra temptation by prohibiting release? *This truly calls upon us to respect the convictions that others have prayerfully weighed before the Lord.*

As spelled out in Lesson 1, God's design for our sexuality is to experience emotional intimacy. However, sexual climax is not the only way to experience connection. For the married, are there other means of deepening your relationship with each other outside of the bedroom? And for the single, be disciplined about staying connected with a core of friends . . . *like maintaining a band.*

May God give you grace and guidance as you form clear convictions on this most difficult issue. And may you extend much grace to others who differ with you.

A Perspective on Victory

Pornography is evil. Period. Sexual addiction and obsession of any kind is energized by dark forces. Make no mistake about it. Whatever your current level of victory or defeat, *press forward!*

Sometimes in the fog of war we lose perspective. Repeated relapses can blur our vision and lull us into apathy. But don't forget all that this bondage has cost you. Determine within your heart not to pass the bondage on to your kids, nor to let it ruin any more relationships.

For many, the approach of this workbook will be absolutely liberating. Some of you may have found one of the prayer keys essential to staying clean. Or possibly you have been infused with strength simply by opening your heart to a band of fellow strugglers. For some, victory is possible by working this program for ninety days.

However, I have worked with sexual addicts for many years and know that some of you will feel this ninety-day effort to be yet another pipedream. You may find a smidgen of healing, but you will feel as condemned as ever to the slavery of sexual obsession.

Do not give up hope! Where God commands obedience, he provides grace to enable us. It simply takes longer for some than for others.

And he has, in fact, commanded obedience for this issue. Likely you already know 1 Thessalonians 4:3: "For this is the will of God, your sanctification: that you abstain from sexual immorality" (ESV). But this verse and others like it are not meant to goad us with guilt. It's not another rock to cram into your knapsack of shame. Not at all.

In fact, at the beginning of this letter, Paul states that this young church had become "an example to all the believers in Macedonia and in Achaia" (1:7). Far from shaming them, Paul had been bragging on them to other churches for how they "turned to God from idols, to serve a living and true God" (1:9)! In chapters 2 and 3, he applauded their courageous faith in the midst of fierce persecution. And even in this fourth chapter, he states that they are living a life that pleases God, but urges them to "do so more and more" (v. 1).

My point? These were sincere believers who had experienced the power of God and, like you, they were seeking to please God. But apparently sexual sin was still very evident among them.

Your progress pleases God. Keep both feet firmly on the path and move forward in faith.

One of my friends recently had a breakthrough. After thirty years (yes, *thirty years*) of crying out to God for consistent victory, he was finally able to avoid pornography week by week. Twelve-step programs, therapy, retreats—he had tried them all. But the one thing he clung to was 1 Thessalonians 4:3: "For this is the will of God, your sanctification: that you abstain from sexual immorality" (ESV). He continued to believe. If God commanded him to abstain from sexual sin, he knew that eventually God would grant him enough healing and strength to have victory.

Perhaps we see this illustrated in Romans 7. No matter what your monkeys, most of us quickly identify with Paul's description. He describes a person who simply cannot do what he knows God wants him to do. His anguish finally finds its voice: "Wretched man that I am! Who will rescue me from this body of death?" (7:24). We find hope, however, from the very next sentence: "Thanks be to God through Jesus Christ our Lord!" (7:25a).

And if you find yourself still in verse 24, take heart! Look to the next chapter and latch onto the following verse with the ferocity of a pit bull: "There is therefore now no condemnation for those who are in Christ Jesus" (Rom. 8:1).

Are you a Christian? Have you found forgiveness for sin? Then the absolute truth is that you are *in Christ Jesus!* There is no condemnation on you! None! Yes, you feel like pond scum. Repeated defeat shouts at you: *"Loser!"* But in God's eyes, each time you humbly cry out for forgiveness, the dust of shame is washed from your feet. All that God sees is the righteousness of Jesus draped over your entire being. That is the truth.

And so, let me be redundantly redundant: *Continue to press forward!*

The principles established in this book are God's means of grace for you. Stay in fellowship with a few safe and trusted friends who can encourage you day by day. Keep the solar panels out, soaking in all of the light of God you can through the prayer exercises and through Scripture reading. Seek inner healing from God through those gifted in formational prayer.

And remember that your sanctification is the work of the Holy Spirit. Continue to ask, seek, and knock for the Holy Spirit to pour out his love into your heart, setting you free from bondage to the flesh (see Luke 11:9–13; Romans 5:1–5).

Press on! Rejoice in God for each new step of progress. Believe with all of your heart that if it is God's will that you abstain from sexual immorality, he will grant sufficient grace and healing to reach ninety days and beyond. Give him no rest as you implore him for the grace to find consistent victory.

The Divine Office for
Sexual Strugglers

The divine office (or daily office) is an ancient devotional practice to consistently connect with God. Some sexual addicts have found this extremely liberating.

All perfectionists, please note: *This is about connection, not completion.* It's merely a tool for you to connect more fully with God. If you don't complete the readings for a certain day, move on! Don't get bogged down. You're on a path of growth, not in a box of obligation.

Cycle One: A Vision for Wholeness

MORNING

Verse of Praise

Sunday: *Know that the* Lᴢᴢᴢ *is God. It is he that made us, and we are his; we are his people, and the sheep of his pasture.* Ps. 100:3

Monday: *"Great and amazing are your deeds, Lord God the Almighty! Just and true are your ways, King of the nations!"* Rev. 15:3

Tuesday: *I praise you, for I am fearfully and wonderfully made. Wonderful are your works; that I know very well.* Ps. 139:14

Wednesday: *"You are worthy, our Lord and God, to receive glory and honor and power, for you created all things, and by your will they existed and were created."* Rev. 4:11

Thursday: *You are a hiding place for me; you preserve me from trouble; you surround me with glad cries of deliverance.* Ps. 32:7

Friday: *May the glory of the* Lᴢᴢᴢ *endure forever; may the* Lᴢᴢᴢ *rejoice in his works.* Ps. 104:31

Saturday: *O give thanks to the* Lᴢᴢᴢ, *for he is good; his steadfast love endures forever!* Ps. 118:1

Daily Morning Confession

We ask your forgiveness, redeeming Lord, for those moments in the night when our hearts were unguarded and wandered into forbidden zones. And we confess the sordidness of impure dreams. Cleanse us for the day before us. Open our hearts to receive your truth from the Scriptures. We commit ourselves to your keeping for this day. In Jesus' name, amen.

Daily Creed

We believe in God the Father, the Maker of heaven and earth, who designed us as male and female to reflect his image. We were made for connection with God and connection with each other. Sexual intimacy provides union with another, the knowing of another, and the possibility of creating others. We were designed to be relationally fulfilled, and sexual intimacy is simply one way to find that fulfillment. Because our genitals are the closest outward connection to the deepest part of our being, sexual touch is to be given and received, not taken or exploited, and only within the security of a covenant.

Scripture Readings (Read one chapter each morning.)

First Week: Genesis 1–3; John 1–4

Second Week: John 5–10; Matthew 19
Third Week: John 11–15; Revelation 21–22

Prayer for Protection

Gracious God, our enemy is persistent, our hearts are deceitful, and our longings are unending. Be our guard. Alert us when Satan has set his snares. Remind us of the costliness of sin. Assure us of your presence and unending love for us. May each member of our band stand firm in their faith, strengthened by your grace, and empowered by your Spirit. To you be the glory! Amen!

EVENING

I will both lie down and sleep in peace; for you alone, O LORD, make me lie down in safety. Ps. 4:8

Confessions for the Day

Most high and holy God: We have become a generation obsessed with sexual satiation. Forgive us for this day's trespasses, when . . .

Our eyes have wandered too far and lingered too long;
Our lips have issued wrongful flirtations and sexual innuendo;

Our hands have reached for inappropriate touch;

Our fingers have clicked on forbidden links;

Our hearts have leaned into ungodly relationships.

Therefore, cleanse us by the blood of Jesus. Dust us off from evil entanglements. Renew and strengthen our deepest desire, which is to honor you with love and obedience. To you be the glory forever! Amen!

Evening Psalm (One each evening.)

First Week: Psalms 1; 2; 8; 18:1–24; 23; 27; 37:1–31

Second Week: Psalms 62; 65; 84; 86; 90; 91; 92

Third Week: Psalms 95; 100; 111; 114; 131; 138; 146

Prayer of Thanksgiving

Thank you, Lord God, for bringing us safely through this day. Thank you for family, friends, and the members of my band. Protect us all from the evil one and evil people. And grant us deep rest this night. In Jesus' name, amen.

Cycle Two: A Perspective on Slipups

MORNING

Verse of Praise

Sunday: *O Lord, you have searched me and known me. You know when I sit down and when I rise up; you discern my thoughts from far away. You search out my path and my lying down, and are acquainted with all my ways.* Ps. 139:1–3

Monday: *Though we stumble, we shall not fall headlong, for the Lord holds us by the hand.* Ps. 37:24

Tuesday: *There is therefore now no condemnation for those who are in Christ Jesus.* Rom. 8:1

Wednesday: *I say to the Lord, "You are my Lord; I have no good apart from you."* . . . *Those who choose another god multiply their sorrows.* Ps. 16:2, 4a

Thursday: *I will render thank offerings to you. For you have delivered my soul from death, and my feet from falling, so that I may walk before God in the light of life.* Ps. 56:12b–13

Friday: *Therefore let all who are faithful offer prayer to you; at a time of distress, the rush of mighty waters shall not reach them.* Ps. 32:6

Saturday: *The LORD upholds all who are falling, and raises up all who are bowed down.* Ps. 145:14

Daily Morning Confession

We ask your forgiveness, redeeming Lord, for those moments in the night when our hearts were unguarded and wandered into forbidden zones. And we confess the sordidness of impure dreams. Cleanse us for the day before us. Open our hearts to receive your truth from the Scriptures. We commit ourselves to your keeping for this day. In Jesus' name, amen.

Daily Creed

We believe the fall greatly distorted our view of reality. Our sinful tendency toward sexuality is expressed in grasping and submitting. We grasp for what is not ours, or we submit to sexuality in idolatrous fashion to meet our needs. This is plainly seen in emotional affairs as the marital bond is adulterated by bonding with another.

God's mission throughout history has been to restore a proper view of him and the world he has created. We find our fulfillment as we surrender our sexuality to Jesus Christ.

Scripture Readings

> First Week: Luke 7; Genesis 37; 39; Judges 14; 15; 16;
> 1 Corinthians 7
>
> Second Week: 2 Samuel 11; 12; 13; Proverbs 5; 6; 7;
> 1 Thessalonians 4
>
> Third Week: Deuteronomy 17:14–23 *with* 1 Kings 10:26–11:13;
> Revelation 2; 3; Romans 3; 6; 7; 8

Prayer for Protection

Gracious God, our enemy is persistent, our hearts are deceitful, and our longings are unending. Be our guard. Alert us when Satan has set his snares. Remind us of the costliness of sin. Assure us of your presence and unending love for us. May each member of our band stand firm in their faith, strengthened by your grace, and empowered by your Spirit. To you be the glory! Amen!

EVENING

I will both lie down and sleep in peace; for you alone, O Lord, make me lie down in safety. Ps. 4:8

Confessions for the Day

Most high and holy God: We have become a generation obsessed with sexual satiation. Forgive us for this day's trespasses, when . . .

Our eyes have wandered too far and lingered too long;

Our lips have issued wrongful flirtations and sexual innuendo;

Our hands have reached for inappropriate touch;

Our fingers have clicked on forbidden links;

Our hearts have leaned into ungodly relationships.

Therefore, cleanse us by the blood of Jesus. Dust us off from evil entanglements. Renew and strengthen our deepest desire, which is to honor you with love and obedience. To you be the glory forever! Amen!

Evening Psalm

First Week: Psalms 18:25–50; 25; 32; 38; 57; 61; 94

Second Week: Psalms 97; 103; 121; 123; 125; 139; 143

Third Week: Psalms 6; 13; 31; 51; 55; 73; 142

Prayer of Thanksgiving

Thank you, Lord God, for bringing us safely through this day. Thank you for family, friends, and the members of my band. Protect us all from the evil one and evil people. And grant us deep rest this night. In Jesus' name, amen.

Cycle Three: A Promise of Freedom

MORNING

Verse of Praise

Sunday: *I lift up my eyes to the hills—from where will my help come? My help comes from the* Lord, *who made heaven and earth.* Ps. 121:1–2

Monday: *This I know, that God is for me. In God, whose word I praise, in the* Lord, *whose word I praise, in God I trust; I am not afraid. What can a mere mortal do to me?* Ps. 56:9b–11

Tuesday: *If God is for us, who is against us? He who did not withhold his own Son, but gave him up for all of us, will he not with him also give us everything else?* Rom. 8:31b–32

Wednesday: *In this is love, not that we loved God but that he loved us and sent his Son to be the atoning sacrifice for our sins.* 1 John 4:10

Thursday: *But thanks be to God, who in Christ always leads us in triumphal procession, and through us spreads in every place the fragrance that comes from knowing him.* 2 Cor. 2:14

Friday: *On the day I called, you answered me, you increased my strength of soul.* Ps. 138:3

Saturday: *I keep the* Lord *always before me; because he is at my right hand, I shall not be moved.* Ps. 16:8

Daily Morning Confession

We ask your forgiveness, redeeming Lord, for those moments in the night when our hearts were unguarded and wandered into forbidden zones. And we confess the sordidness of impure dreams. Cleanse us for the day before us. Open our hearts to receive your truth from the Scriptures. We commit ourselves to your keeping for this day. In Jesus' name, amen.

Daily Creed

To redeem a world of grasping and idolatrous submission, Jesus emptied himself of the privileges of heaven and submitted to the plan of the Father. We live in a time between gardens characterized by "already and not yet." Healing and restoration of sexual brokenness is already available, but not yet in all of its fullness. As disciples of Jesus Christ, we must deny ourselves of the idolatrous responses of addiction and aversion, seek the healing God offers, and await the fulfillment of all things in the garden of paradise.

Scripture Readings

First Week: Isaiah 41; 42:1–9; 49:14–26; 53; 54; 61; 65:17–25
Second Week: Luke 10; 14; 15; 18; 19; 22:31–62; 23:26–24:12
Third Week: 1 Peter 1–5; 1 John 1; 4

Prayer for Protection

Gracious God, our enemy is persistent, our hearts are deceitful, and our longings are unending. Be our guard. Alert us when Satan has set his snares. Remind us of the costliness of sin. Assure us of your presence and unending love for us. May each member of our band stand firm in their faith, strengthened by your grace, and empowered by your Spirit. To you be the glory! Amen!

EVENING

I will both lie down and sleep in peace; for you alone, O LORD, make me lie down in safety. Ps. 4:8

Confessions for the Day

Most high and holy God: We have become a generation obsessed with sexual satiation. Forgive us for this day's trespasses, when . . .

Our eyes have wandered too far and lingered too long;
Our lips have issued wrongful flirtations and sexual innuendo;
Our hands have reached for inappropriate touch;
Our fingers have clicked on forbidden links;
Our hearts have leaned into ungodly relationships.

Therefore, cleanse us by the blood of Jesus. Dust us off from evil entanglements. Renew and strengthen our deepest desire, which is to honor you with love and obedience. To you be the glory forever! Amen!

Evening Psalm

First Week: Psalms 4; 12; 14; 17; 24; 26; 28

Second Week: Psalms 34; 42; 50; 52; 53; 56; 60

Third Week: Psalms 80; 96; 98; 105:1–22; 107; 112; 147

Prayer of Thanksgiving

Thank you, Lord God, for bringing us safely through this day. Thank you for family, friends, and the members of my band. Protect us all from the evil one and evil people. And grant us deep rest this night. In Jesus' name, amen.

Cycle Four: A Vision for the Church

MORNING

Verse of Praise

Sunday: *Who will separate us from the love of Christ? Will hardship, or distress, or persecution, or famine, or nakedness, or peril, or sword? . . .*

No, in all these things we are more than conquerors through him who loved us. Rom. 8:35, 37

Monday: *But they have conquered [Satan] by the blood of the Lamb and by the word of their testimony, for they did not cling to life even in the face of death.* Rev. 12:11

Tuesday: *The LORD will fulfill his purpose for me; your steadfast love, O LORD, endures forever.* Ps. 138:8

Wednesday: *It is he whom we proclaim, warning everyone and teaching everyone in all wisdom, so that we may present everyone mature in Christ. For this I toil and struggle with all the energy that he powerfully inspires within me.* Col. 1:28–29

Thursday: *The law of the LORD is perfect, reviving the soul; the decrees of the LORD are sure, making wise the simple; the precepts of the LORD are right, rejoicing the heart; the commandment of the LORD is clear, enlightening the eyes.* Ps. 19:7–8

Friday: *I cry to God Most High, to God who fulfills his purpose for me.* Ps. 57:2

Saturday: *But I do not count my life of any value to myself, if only I may finish my course and the ministry that I received from the Lord Jesus, to testify to the good news of God's grace.* Acts 20:24

Daily Morning Confession

We ask your forgiveness, redeeming Lord, for those moments in the night when our hearts were unguarded and wandered into forbidden zones. And we confess the sordidness of impure dreams. Cleanse us for the day before us. Open our hearts to receive your truth from the Scriptures. We commit ourselves to your keeping for this day. In Jesus' name, amen.

Daily Creed

We believe in the church universal, the bride of Christ, even with all of its spots, wrinkles, and blemishes. The church is the body of Christ called to serve as the hands and feet of Jesus among the last, the least, and the lost. A bruised and bleeding world waits for us to be a safe and healing sanctuary for all who are cloistered in closets of shame. The gates of hell are powerless against a united and equipped people of God.

We believe the Bible presents a consistent theology of sexuality. God's template for sexual expression was shaped in the garden of Eden, affirmed by the teachings of Jesus, redeemed at Calvary, and will find its fulfillment in the garden of paradise. The boundaries for sexual behavior are clear: a lifelong loving bond that is monogamous, heterosexual, and covenantal.

Scripture Readings

> First Week: Acts 1–7
>
> Second Week: Leviticus 18; 19; 20; Matthew 5; 6; 7;
>   Ephesians 5
>
> Third Week: Acts 14; 15; 16; 17; 19; 1 Corinthians 9;
>   2 Corinthians 4

Prayer for Protection

Gracious God, our enemy is persistent, our hearts are deceitful, and our longings are unending. Be our guard. Alert us when Satan has set his snares. Remind us of the costliness of sin. Assure us of your presence and unending love for us. May each member of our band stand firm in their faith, strengthened by your grace, and empowered by your Spirit. To you be the glory! Amen!

EVENING

I will both lie down and sleep in peace; for you alone, O LORD, make me lie down in safety. Ps. 4:8

Confessions for the Day

Most high and holy God: We have become a generation obsessed with sexual satiation. Forgive us for this day's trespasses, when . . .

Our eyes have wandered too far and lingered too long;

Our lips have issued wrongful flirtations and sexual innuendo;

Our hands have reached for inappropriate touch;

Our fingers have clicked on forbidden links;

Our hearts have leaned into ungodly relationships.

Therefore, cleanse us by the blood of Jesus. Dust us off from evil entanglements. Renew and strengthen our deepest desire, which is to honor you with love and obedience. To you be the glory forever! Amen!

Evening Psalm

First Week: Psalms 3; 5; 9; 15; 16; 19; 20

Second Week: Psalms 21; 30; 33; 46; 63; 67; 71

Third Week: Psalms 75; 76; 82; 85; 88; 93; 130

Fourth Week: Psalms 108; 110; 116; 118; 133; 148; 150

Prayer of Thanksgiving

Thank you, Lord God, for bringing us safely through this day. Thank you for family, friends, and the members of my band. Protect us all from the evil one and evil people. And grant us deep rest this night. In Jesus' name, amen.

CPSIA information can be obtained
at www.ICGtesting.com
Printed in the USA
LVHW031154220221
679551LV00005B/6

9 781628 248333